RECOVERING from NARCISSISTIC MOTHERS

RECOVERING
from
NARCISSISTIC MOTHERS

A DAUGHTER'S WORKBOOK

Ellen Biros, MS, LCSW, C-PD

ROCKRIDGE PRESS

First Rockridge Press trade paperback edition 2022

Rockridge Press and the Rockridge Press logo are trademarks or registered trademarks of Callisto Media Inc. and/or its affiliates in the United States and other countries and may not be used without written permission.

For general information on our other products and services, please contact our Customer Care Department within the United States at (866) 744-2665, or outside the United States at (510) 253-0500.

Paperback ISBN: 978-1-63878-407-4 | eBook ISBN: 978-1-63878-520-0

Manufactured in the United States of America

Interior and Cover Designer: Monica Cheng
Art Producer: Janice Ackerman
Editor: Mo Mozuch
Production Manager: Jose Olivera

All illustrations used under license from iStock
Author photo courtesy of Brian Tisdale

10 9 8 7 6 5 4 3 2 1 0

*For my mother, Carol, and
my daughters, Sam and Quinn,
for teaching me how to
love unconditionally.*

Contents

Introduction

How does one describe the importance of our relationship with our mothers? This relationship is arguably one of the most important relationships we will have in our lifetime. It also sets the stage for all other relationships moving forward. It's a template, if you will; a guide from which all other relationships will be formed.

At its healthiest, the mother-daughter relationship embodies compassion, security, stability, love, and support. At its unhealthiest, it sets in motion a series of problems, including unstable relationships, self-hatred, boundarylessness, and more, which can follow a daughter around for the course of her life. By picking up this workbook, you have opened yourself to the possibilities that come with healing. By learning to love yourself and gaining a better understanding of your relationship with your mother, you will develop a healthy mindset and increase your confidence and ability to manage all relationships in your life.

My name is Ellen Biros, and I am a licensed clinical social worker and personality disorder specialist. I've been working as a therapist and social worker for over twenty-five years. While in private practice, I saw a pattern emerging with women seeking therapy to find out "what was wrong" with them. My clients consistently asked, "Am I crazy?" or "Am I too sensitive, emotional, or angry?" There was indeed a connection—they had all been told by the person tasked with protecting them that there was something wrong with them. As a result, their perceptions of themselves were warped, their relationships in tatters, and their mental health hanging perilously by a thread. They were struggling in almost all parts of their lives. Initially, their issues seemed to be with their partners, but as we began our therapeutic work, it became clear that the main purveyors of their abuse were their mothers.

I have frequently recommended that clients use workbooks, both as a support between sessions and as a means of processing issues during sessions. However, I had a difficult time finding a workbook that could support a daughter working through issues of narcissistic abuse at the hands of her mother. So, as I worked with my clients who were struggling to understand the complicated dynamics of their relationship with their mothers, I utilized a hodgepodge of exercises that I customized to address issues specific to daughters of narcissistic mothers. This workbook contains the exercises that I found to be most helpful in assisting my clients.

Therapists frequently encourage clients to journal, write, research, and understand the issues they are working through. Workbook exercises offer a productive way to work through the difficult emotions, memories, and experiences that can be debilitating after abuse. Hopefully, you'll find that the information and exercises in this workbook help you begin to unravel the tangled web of abuse. Childhood narcissistic abuse robs you of your self-esteem and ability to trust. In contrast, healing and recovery allow you to discover your identity and figure out who you are, what you value, and where your path leads. Healing begins with understanding what has happened to you and how it affects your life as an adult. The strength you used to survive your abuse is the strength you will draw on to recover.

I strongly encourage all readers to seek out therapy, support groups, or psychiatric care if you find yourself having difficulty regulating your emotions or are unable to perform the tasks of daily life. This workbook is not meant to take the place of seeing a therapist, taking medication, or seeking medical treatment.

How to Use This Book

This workbook is arranged in two parts. Part 1 consists of two chapters that outline how to recognize a narcissistic mother and explore what it's like to grow up with a narcissistic mother. Part 2 includes four chapters of workbook exercises, practices, prompts, and affirmations. You'll also find relatable case studies throughout this workbook, which are fictionalized accounts loosely based on actual client experiences.

Each chapter will focus on a different theme, ranging from understanding and processing your emotions around experiencing the abuse of a narcissistic mother to learning to break the cycle of abuse and heal your relationship with yourself, your mother, and all others you spend time with.

The chapters are designed to help you process your abuse in a supportive, reflective, and healing manner. To get the most out of this workbook, I recommend working through every chapter from start to finish. You may find that you work on specific exercises out of order or take more time with one exercise than another. This is all fine! This is your process and your recovery. Each daughter's journey is unique.

I encourage you to show yourself grace and compassion as you work through the book. You may work on the exercises intently for a while and then find you need to take a break. There is no time limit on healing. Go at your own pace and do what you can. If at any time you feel you need professional support, please don't hesitate to contact a licensed mental health provider. You can do this—let's go!

PART ONE

RECOGNIZING THE NARCISSISTIC MOTHER

This is the first part of your journey toward recovery. You may have selected this workbook because you are curious whether your mother is or was a narcissist. Perhaps you selected this workbook because you realize that your mother did not give you the unconditional love that you deserved. For whatever reason you chose this book, welcome.

Before immersing ourselves in the workbook activities and exercises, we'll explore what it means to be raised by a narcissistic mother. Part 1 will help you begin to learn about yourself and your mother. It may not be an easy trip, but you'll discover how difficult emotions, disappointment, and feelings of inadequacy have shaped your life. Starting with an overview of narcissism, this portion will explain the origins of narcissism and help you identify whether your mother exhibits or exhibited narcissistic traits. You'll learn about different types of narcissism and examine how the tactics of a narcissistic mother create debilitating symptoms in a daughter and impact the mother-daughter relationship in the long term. At the end of part 1, you'll have a strong grasp on how to identify narcissistic characteristics, how they can develop, and what effects they have on the relationship between mother and daughter.

"These incessantly disapproving voices never gave me a moment's peace. They harangued, nagged, and demeaned me with the overall message that no matter how hard I tried, I could never succeed, could never be good enough."

—KARYL MCBRIDE, PhD

CHAPTER ONE

What Is Narcissistic Personality Disorder?

It seems the term "narcissism" is everywhere these days. The term is used loosely to describe anyone who is arrogant or selfish, but is that all there is to it? Defining narcissistic personality disorder can be tricky. It's generally described as a mental health disorder defined by glaring self-absorption and excessive cravings for admiration. Narcissism is a complex problem, so understanding its traits is essential.

Likely, you have experienced the abuse that children of narcissistic parents endure. You may have felt confused, invalidated, and unloved. Perhaps you believed that your mother's behavior was normal, or maybe you even blamed yourself for her behavior. Due to the insidious nature of narcissistic abuse and the narcissist's ability to create a false persona, she often escapes accountability. This is why it's so important to learn to put into words what has been done to you. Narcissists are so good at employing a dizzying array of behaviors that you may not realize you have been abused. It is only after learning to identify the covert ways narcissists abuse that you can truly achieve recovery.

"I define narcissism as the shame-based fear of being ordinary."

—BRENÉ BROWN

Defining Narcissism

The term "narcissism" originates from a myth about a young Greek man named Narcissus. Handsome and vain, Narcissus fell in love with his own reflection in a pool of water. He was unable to pull himself away from his reflection and ultimately died from thirst. In modern times, a narcissist is someone we identify as self-absorbed and arrogant.

The *Diagnostic and Statistical Manual of Mental Disorders* (DSM-5-TR) describes narcissistic personality disorder, or NPD, as a disorder in a cluster of personality disorders defined as dramatic, emotional, and erratic. It lists nine characteristics of narcissism:

1. Possesses an overblown sense of self-importance

2. Obsessed with achieving success, power, and the perfect mate

3. Believes they are superior to others and will only associate with other superior people

4. Needs constant reassurance and validation

5. Believes they are inherently deserving of special privileges or treatment

6. Will take advantage of other people's vulnerabilities to get what they want

7. Lacks empathy; cannot see other's perspectivess

8. Desires what others have and believes others are envious of them

9. Comes across as conceited, boastful, and arrogant

These combined traits lead the narcissist, and specifically the narcissistic mother, to present themselves as though everything in life is perfect. However, the daughter of a narcissistic mother will tell you this is all a facade. In private, narcissists are unpredictable, with a propensity toward impatience and rage, leaving family members guessing what will happen next.

NARCISSISM IN MODERN LIFE

The prevalence of NPD is a much-debated topic. Some research suggests that it's not as widespread as believed by the general public. The prevalence according to the DSM-5-TR is projected to be up to 6 percent of the population. Research published in the *Journal of Clinical Psychiatry* suggests that the rate for men (7.7 percent) is higher than for women (4.8 percent).

It can be difficult to collect valid and reliable data on the pervasiveness of the disorder because people with NPD do not regularly seek out treatment on their own. Most often, people with narcissism seek out therapy or treatment as mandated by the legal system, their employer, or their partner to avoid facing a consequence (divorce, unemployment, legal problems, etc.). If they do follow through with treatment, they often withdraw when faced with confrontation or if they feel backed into a corner.

It seems that narcissism has become more prevalent over the past few decades. In recent years, the so-called "self-esteem movement," intended to build up self-esteem in children, actually created a generation of emotionally fragile kids and young adults. It turns out that sheltering children from adverse consequences and experiences, rather than teaching them the importance of resilience and hard work, inflates their egos. Additionally, the rise of social media and reality TV has brought about an increase in the perceived importance of fame, wealth, celebrity, and the superficial. These factors can influence our view of ourselves and what we value. All this appears to have led us to a society of "me, me, me," which is a perfect breeding environment for a narcissist.

What Causes NPD?

The causes of narcissism are not entirely clear; however, they are likely a combination of genetic, environmental, and other psychological factors. It's commonly believed that narcissism develops as a result of problematic parenting. Individuals whose parents invalidated or rejected them appear to struggle in adult life with self-esteem and self-worth. Conversely, too much praise and admiration in childhood can also lead to narcissism. Parental overvaluing may encourage an overly positive view of self in children. This leads to feelings of inferiority when the grandiose perception is not supported in the outside world. Research suggests that narcissism can also be the result of genetics (see "Gene Abnormality," page 10). Regardless of the cause, narcissists go on to construct unhealthy, abusive, and destructive relationships. Let's take a more detailed look at the possible contributors to narcissism.

Insensitive Parenting

Insensitive parenting, sometimes referred to as indifferent or neglectful parenting, is characterized by a lack of awareness or sensitivity to a child's needs. Insensitive parents show very little love, affection, or support to their children. They may have limited interaction with their children, set few expectations, and not involve themselves in their child's school or extracurricular activities. Consequently, children whose parents are neglectful have a difficult time setting boundaries, lack self-identity, and struggle with forming relationships throughout their lives. Children of insensitive parents may struggle with overwhelming emotions, have difficulty learning appropriate behaviors, and are more likely to misbehave.

Excessive Pampering or Praise

The term "helicopter parenting" is a common descriptor of parents who overvalue their children's achievements. Although it's healthy to praise a child's well-earned accomplishments, it's another thing to celebrate non-accomplishments or behaviors that should occur as a natural part of learning responsibility. When parents lead their children to believe that they are more deserving than others, it can cause a child to feel that other people are beneath them. When a child is rewarded for every behavior and does not experience consequences or discomfort in life, an overinflated ego can result. A sense of superiority and a lack of empathy, both hallmarks of narcissism, can lead to serious consequences in both childhood and adulthood.

Excessive Criticism

A parent, and specifically a mother, has an enormous responsibility to their child: helping them develop a healthy sense of self and self-esteem. As children, we believe everything our parents tell us, good and bad. Children of excessively critical parents will believe the negative feedback and absorb it like a sponge, leaving them to struggle with their identity. Excessive criticism is always detrimental, particularly to a young child and especially when it comes from a child's caregivers. This will lead a child to question their worth and validity for a lifetime and sets the stage for them to develop pathological ways of developing self-esteem. They may develop a "special" role in the family system, and as they begin to assert their role as "special," the grandiose self is the only way to gain attention and approval.

Trauma

Trauma can be a complicated concept. Simply put, trauma is an isolated or ongoing negative event that changes the functioning of our day-to-day lives. This couldn't be truer than for a child who grows up in an abusive family. The insecure, inconsistent, unpredictable daily life of a child who experiences abuse and trauma changes the child's nervous system and makes it difficult to regulate itself. The result is a child who is overstimulated and unable to calm themselves, waiting for the next round of chaos to begin. Abuse robs a child of their ability to develop a sense of identity, self-esteem, and ego strength. As they move into adulthood, they can develop narcissistic traits as they look for admiration and validation from others.

Extremely High Expectations

Some parents see their children as extensions of themselves, making it difficult to separate their own failures from their children's. Every child seeks attention and approval from their parents, but when a parent's approval is tied to who they want the child to be rather than who the child is as an individual, this can impact the child for a lifetime. When parents have extremely high expectations for their child, the child focuses only on their parents' reaction. The child is left to develop their identity based on what their parents think rather than what they think about themselves. Their sense of identity then becomes dependent on what they achieve. As an adult, their only value is achievement, and they begin to devalue anyone who does not see how special and successful they are.

Gene Abnormality

Years ago, there was very little research on whether personality disorders might be genetic or inherited. In other words, do we inherit personality problems from our family, or is there a gene mutation to account for them?

According to a study conducted by Luo, Cai, and Song, both grandiosity and entitlement were found to be characteristics of narcissism that can be inherited from your parents. Grandiosity is the characteristic of finding oneself superior to all others; entitlement is a belief that you are inherently deserving of privilege and special treatment. Other studies suggest that there may be X chromosome involvement (the chromosome you inherit from both your mother and your father) and that people with narcissistic personality disorder have less gray matter in their brain, an area linked to empathy.

Rashima's Trauma Triumph

Rashima, a fifty-five-year-old woman and a successful attorney, is divorced from a narcissistic husband and has two children now in their mid-twenties. Rashima was married to her ex-husband for over twenty years; it took a long time to realize he was abusive, but she felt empowered when she divorced him and was finally "free." Soon after the divorce was finalized, Rashima felt as if she might be ready to date again but began having apprehensions. She went on a couple of dates but couldn't seem to shake the overwhelming feeling of doubt and uncertainty.

Rashima decided to seek out her previous therapist, who helped her work through her initial feelings after the divorce. After talking with her therapist, Rashima realized she was struggling with trauma. She confided that she had never admitted she was abused. She struggled with doubt about her perceptions of what happened in her marriage. As the discussion went on, Rashima revealed that her mother had been overly critical of her when she was a child. Her mother did not allow Rashima to share her feelings. If Rashima tried to talk about how she was feeling, her mother would shut the conversation down, claiming that she had other things to tend to. Rashima believed that her mother's comments were true, that her concerns and problems weren't important and she didn't deserve her mother's time or attention.

Rashima began to realize that the problems with her mother were some of the same problems she had with her ex-husband. Her mother had narcissistic traits. As Rashima came to fully understand narcissism, she realized the truth: Her mother's behavior was not Rashima's fault. This relieved a great burden, one that Rashima had been carrying around since she was a child. Suddenly, she felt "free" once again!

Identifying NPD in Others

As we've discussed, narcissistic people have an inflated sense of themselves, demand attention and admiration from others, and struggle with relationships due to a lack of empathy. The DSM-5-TR suggests that five of the following characteristics should be present to diagnose narcissism:

1. Possesses a grandiose sense of self-importance (always talks about herself and never asks about you)

2. Fantasizes of unlimited success, power, brilliance, beauty, or ideal love (tells exaggerated stories that don't make sense about winning homecoming queen, dating the football captain, or winning a beauty contest)

3. Believes they are special and should only associate with people who can appreciate them or are of high status (refuses to attend your birthday party because the attention won't be on her)

4. Requires excessive admiration (demands praise and compliments for everything she has ever done for you)

5. Possesses a sense of entitlement (believes standing in line is beneath her)

6. Manipulates and takes advantage of others (only associates with people who can "do something" for her)

7. Lacks empathy (always criticizes and corrects you)

8. Envies others and believes others are envious of them (believes all women are jealous of her)

9. Behaves in an arrogant and haughty manner (disapproves of those who have fewer material possessions)

Not all narcissists display the same characteristics. Depending on the person, someone may show only a couple of these traits, while another may exhibit all nine. Although only a licensed professional can diagnose the disorder, it may be helpful to explore some common traits expressed by the narcissistic mother.

Opportunistic

Narcissists are opportunists. They exploit the vulnerabilities of others to gain something for themselves. Who is more vulnerable than a child? Narcissistic mothers often take advantage of their daughters to make themselves more appealing to others. Because of the power disparity in parent-child relationships, narcissistic mothers who exploit their daughters for their own personal gains are particularly ruthless. A lack of boundaries creates an environment that makes it difficult or impossible for a daughter to say no or learn that it's acceptable to protect herself.

Disconnected from Reality

Narcissists are focused on showing other people how wonderful they are. Narcissistic people live in a fantasy world in which they are the star of the show and others are around to serve them. This is certainly the case with the narcissistic mother. A daughter is the ultimate extension of the narcissist mother. A narcissistic mother will invite her daughter into her own dreams and fantasies, leaving a daughter to focus all of her attention on her mother. When the narcissistic mother's fantasies come crashing down, a daughter is left to pick up all of the pieces, trading roles and making every effort to reassure her mother that all will be fine again.

Manipulative

Narcissists are master manipulators. They know exactly how to sway the emotions of their victims to get what they want. Since daughters are in a uniquely vulnerable position with narcissistic mothers, it doesn't take much to control and gain influence. Who knows you better than your mother? She has known everything about you since you were born. She knows every button to push and every insecurity. Narcissistic mothers will use this knowledge to shame and guilt a daughter into getting what she wants. If she senses any resistance, she will stop at nothing to pressure you to feel guilty for your lack of allegiance.

Envious

For most mothers, a child's success, intellect, talent, or beauty is a source of pride and joy. For a narcissistic mother, it's a source of jealousy and envy. As we have learned, narcissism can develop as a result of abuse and neglect. When a child doesn't receive the attention and love of a parent, she may begin to acquire and collect material things to fill that void and gain the attention and affection of others. This places her in two competing roles at once: one, as the exceptional child who others should envy, but also as the daughter who can't dazzle too brightly and outshine her mother.

Superior

Narcissists spend their lives trying to convince themselves and others that they are worthy. In doing so, they believe that they are superior to all others. A narcissistic mother believes she is the smartest, most beautiful, and wealthiest person in the room. Any attention she receives is considered proof of her superiority. In her tireless efforts to maintain this facade, she will align herself with others who can help her fill this role, even at the cost of her daughter. Watching your mother try to connect with someone else while ignoring you is one of the most damaging experiences in life. It is important to remember that you are good enough and you always have been!

Pretentious

While the narcissist works diligently to convince herself that she is superior, she must also convince others. To present the illusion of superiority, the narcissistic mother must show tangible proof. Enrolling her daughter in the best schools, driving the best car, or living in the chicest neighborhood will garner the admiration and validation she is seeking. Narcissistic mothers will go into debt, max out credit cards, and go into bankruptcy, all in the name of protecting the illusion. Unfortunately, she has modeled for her daughter lying, deceitfulness, and manipulation as a normal part of life.

Materialistic

Narcissistic mothers are materialistic. A narcissist must have the latest designer accessories and the highest priced items, for both herself and her daughter. She needs these possessions to validate her high status and believes these items will help fill the void she feels. These material items are her security blanket, but what is best today will not be good enough tomorrow. As soon as someone has seen her new dress or her new purse, the emptiness and fear return, prompting her to acquire more new items, again and again.

Non-Empathetic

The ability to place yourself in someone else's shoes and share the feelings of another person is an important trait. Narcissists lack this skill, but they *have* perfected the art of *pretending* to have empathetic feelings. A narcissistic mother who expresses concern that her friend can't join her for lunch because she isn't feeling well is simply upset that she won't be able to show off her new handbag rather than concerned for the well-being of her friend. Her daughter may not want to see this for what it is; after all, we want to see our mothers as loving, caring, and compassionate toward others.

Do any of these traits sound familiar? The quiz that follows will help you better understand if your mother exhibits narcissistic characteristics.

Does or Did Your Mother Exhibit Narcissistic Traits?

Narcissistic mothers may possess any number of the following traits. Take your time as you reflect on the following questions.

1. Is/was your mother overly concerned with what others think? _Yes_

2. Do you feel like your mother is/was trying to compete with you? _Yes_

3. Do you feel like your mother lacks/lacked empathy for your feelings and situations? _Yes!_

4. Does/did your mother do things for you, praise you, and support you only when others are/were around? _Yes_

5. Are you unclear about whether your mother likes/liked or loves/loved you? _Yes!_

6. Does/did your mother fail to take responsibility for her feelings and actions and blame things on you or others? _Yes!!_

7. Has your mother gone silent or carried a grudge for a long time rather than resolving the problem? _Yes!!!_

8. Do/did you feel like you are/were responsible for your mother's emotional well-being? _Yes!_

9. When you accomplish something, is your first thought "What will/would my mother think?" _Yes!_

10. Does/did your mother act like a victim or martyr when she didn't get her way? _Yes!_

Note: All of these questions relate to characteristics of narcissism. The more questions that you answered yes to, the higher the likelihood that your mother has traits of a narcissist. Please note that only licensed professionals can give a formal diagnosis for narcissistic personality disorder.

The Different Narcissistic Profiles

We've explored general descriptions of a person with NPD, but clinicians and mental health professionals use variations to classify narcissists. Like most psychiatric disorders, narcissism may include several different forms and levels of severity. Although there are anywhere from three to ten variations of narcissistic profiles, one thing is for sure: No two narcissists are exactly alike. The following variations are not considered to be diagnoses but can help break down specific behaviors and nuances of the narcissist as well as explain how to respond or rationalize in times of conflict.

Communal Narcissist

Narcissists have an increased sense of superiority and entitlement, and their lack of empathy makes it difficult or impossible for them to be genuinely concerned about the needs and concerns of others. Communal narcissists value holding important roles in a community. Although their involvement may seem altruistic, this role is actually self-serving to the narcissist. The more attention they receive, the more it boosts their ego. They promote themselves by boasting about their extraordinary ability to listen and connect with others. Having an extreme dedication to a charity or cause or discussing their commitment to a calling is a sign of communal narcissism. These narcissists may try to make you feel selfish or demanding if you ask for their attention, but asking for help is a critical skill for self-care and is never a selfish act.

Covert Narcissist *This one!*

Perhaps the most difficult type of narcissist to identify, covert narcissists fly under the radar. They may present as vulnerable or fragile but are secretly grandiose and jealous. Covert narcissists use guilt and blame to stay in control. Although they may initially appear gracious and kind, there is an underlying motive: to accumulate praise and admiration. Dealing with a covert narcissist's manipulative behaviors can make you feel like you are responsible for taking care of their emotional well-being. Remember, a narcissist of any type behaves in negative ways because of an issue with them, not you. Don't let them gaslight you or skew your reality. Focus objectively on whether you contributed negatively to an interaction rather than the narcissist's view of the interaction.

Malignant Narcissist

The malignant narcissistic mother is the cruelest of mothers: vicious, aggressive, and deliberate in her abuse. A narcissistic mother derives pleasure from the pain she inflicts. She will give your beloved pet away just to hurt you. She'll require you to do all the household chores and then berate you when they're not done perfectly. If you say something that she perceives as embarrassing, she will say you're thoughtless, stupid, and selfish. Daughters of malignant narcissistic mothers develop survival skills. The more traits of malignant narcissism, the more dangerous she will be. Remember, you can't fix a narcissist. You can only learn to protect yourself.

COMMON NPD MYTHS

Myth: *All narcissists are men.*

Truth: *Most people who are diagnosed with narcissistic personality disorder are men; however, research suggests that 4.8 percent of women have diagnosable symptoms of the disorder.*

Myth: *Narcissists have high self-esteem.*

Truth: *Narcissists do not have a stable sense of self-esteem; it's completely dependent on the validation of others. Narcissists rely on others to help them regulate their self-esteem while having no interest in reciprocating.*

Myth: *People with some narcissistic traits must have narcissistic personality disorder.*

Truth: *It's easy to think that people who are self-centered or unempathetic have this disorder. The reality is that many people may have mild traits associated with narcissism but do not meet the clinical criteria for the personality disorder.*

Myth: *All narcissists want to hurt people.*

Truth: *Although most people in relationships with narcissists end up getting hurt, narcissists usually do not intend to hurt others. In fact, because of their lack of empathy, they usually are not thinking about the feelings of others at all. They are wrapped up in their own world and their need to seek validation and admiration from others.*

Myth: *Social media causes narcissism.*

Truth: *Social media can feed the needs of a narcissist and is a favored tool for some narcissists, but it's not the cause of narcissism. As we've explored, the cause of narcissism is unknown, but trauma, genetics, and parenting factors in a child's life are more likely involved in the actual development of the disorder.*

A Narcissistic Mother's Tactics of Choice

The possibility that a parent would use an arsenal of tools and tactics against their child is unthinkable. However, narcissistic mothers employ a multitude of different methods to manipulate and control their daughters. A narcissistic mother's inability to provide a safe and secure environment for her child leads them down a road of self-doubt, indecisiveness, and codependency. Narcissistic mothers relate to their daughters by utilizing control, deflection, distortion, and projection. After growing up in an environment without boundaries and being told she's being selfish for trying to protect herself, a daughter is left susceptible to continued abuse as an adult because she believes she is the problem.

Lack of Boundaries

Boundaries are valuable tools we can use to protect ourselves. Most of us learn these boundaries from our parents or caretakers. The forced role of a daughter of a narcissistic mother is to protect her mother, not herself. The lack of boundaries in a mother-daughter relationship creates enmeshment; it becomes difficult to identify where one person ends and the other begins. The daughter lives with no privacy, constant demands for her time and energy, and blurred roles. Is my mother my friend, or am I her parent?

Toxic Shame

Shame and guilt are common emotions for the daughter of a narcissistic mother. But shame is believing that the problem is you. The narcissistic mother's goal is to ensure that her daughter never grows independent enough to recognize Mom's need for constant admiration and validation. She will shame her daughter for not accomplishing academically, socially, or professionally and for having any of her own original thoughts, ideas, or expressions. These are all threats to the maternal narcissist's control, and the repression of her individualism ultimately leaves a daughter with a sense of never being good enough.

Control

Control is the root of the narcissistic mother's behavior. All narcissists have an instinctive need to control every aspect of their lives because not having control means the risk of narcissistic injury. Narcissistic injury occurs when the narcissist's fragile ego is threatened. Their vulnerable self-esteem makes them very sensitive to criticism or abandonment. What better person to help shield their ego than a daughter who is dependent on her mother's protection? The narcissistic mother has no shame in using controlling behaviors to get her way, and the more she uses control, the more normalized it becomes for her daughter.

Competition

What's it like to be in constant competition with the person who is supposed to be helping you become an independent, confident woman? The daughter of a narcissistic mother knows this feeling. A narcissistic woman may view *all* women as competition. The narcissistic mother may criticize her daughter's appearance or body and demand physical perfection. The daughter of a maternal narcissist faces jealousy and envy from the person who is supposed to build her up and support her transition into adulthood.

Emotional Disconnect

Although a narcissistic mother may be physically present with her daughter, she's emotionally unavailable. She may be unable to express love or affection and doesn't ask about or validate her child's emotions. When a parent is emotionally distant or disconnected, the child is left to navigate the world on their own. Humans are inherently emotional beings. We thrive on the connections we make with others, and if this connection isn't encouraged in children, they aren't able to relate to others. Narcissistic mothers are masters at "intermittent attention" as well. When a daughter gets only fragmented attention from her mother, she learns that she must perform to get her mother's attention—sometimes achieving it and sometimes failing.

Key Takeaways

Give yourself a round of applause! You made it through the first chapter of your workbook. With that, you're on the road to recovery. Although it may be difficult at times to understand and you may still be digesting a great deal of what you have read, hang in there. Now you have a starter kit for recovery. As you move through this workbook, you'll begin to understand that narcissism and the behaviors associated with it have nothing to do with you.

It can help to remember the following:

→ Narcissistic personality disorder is a clinical psychiatric disorder. The behaviors of the narcissist result from the disorder, not from the behaviors of other people.

→ The specific causes of narcissism are a combination of genetic, environmental, and psychological factors.

→ Narcissism exists on a spectrum and can consist of different nuances and behaviors.

→ Understanding how narcissism develops is the first step in the healing process. Arming yourself with information can help you recognize what you did not receive as a child and will help you create a template for healing.

CHAPTER TWO

Growing Up with an NPD Mother

The relationship between a mother and her daughter can be one of the most complicated but fulfilling relationships we have. A mother is a role model, and her behavior during formative years can affect a daughter's self-esteem, sense of identity, and ability to form meaningful relationships throughout her life.

Consider the responsibility bestowed on a mother when she first meets her daughter. With a healthy mother, all of the dreams and wishes she has for her daughter will come to fruition as the daughter gets older. When a daughter has a narcissist for a mother, she faces challenges that stunt her ability to develop in a healthy way. In this chapter, we will identify some of those challenges and what it means to grow up with a narcissistic mother. A child who grows up in a home with a lack of nurturing and struggles with feelings of emptiness and guilt spends their life searching for their identity. We will be exploring some difficult concepts that may seem overwhelming at times. Stay strong and remember, identifying the dynamics will lead to a better understanding of how you can heal.

"We may encounter many defeats, but we must not be defeated. It may be necessary to encounter the defeat, so that we can know who we are. So that we can see, oh, that happened, and I rose. I did get knocked down flat in front of the whole world, and I rose."

—MAYA ANGELOU

Understanding the Mother–Daughter Relationship

Bonding and attachment occur between mother and child when the child's needs are consistently met. By responding with love, care, and warmth to a baby's needs, the mother establishes a trusting bond. When a child receives a touch, a smile, or a snuggle, the world is a safe and trustworthy place. This begins the vital foundation for healthy development.

Research suggests that the development of empathy is one of the critical components to the successful emotional and social development of children. A parent's ability to respond to the emotional signals of their child is essential for survival. However, narcissistic mothers do not have this response. A mother who lacks empathy and compassion fails to bond with her child and meets the child's needs only when it's in the mother's best interest. The child learns that they are unable to depend on their mother and grows up fearing abandonment and yearning for that connection they didn't receive. This increases the likelihood of choosing relationships that are abusive and self-serving in adulthood.

When the Child Becomes the Parent

Children who grow up in homes in which one or both parents are abusive, neglectful, or substance-abusing take on the role of the responsible adult. This phenomenon, called parentification, occurs when the child is expected to take care of the physical and emotional needs of the parent.

The daughter of a narcissistic mother is placed in an impossible position. She does not have the capacity, wisdom, or intellectual development to meet her mother's needs, yet she must deal with her narcissistic mother's rage. She will do anything to please or gain acceptance from her mother in the hopes of some connection or attention.

Role reversal has detrimental effects on a child's development. The daughter should be learning to take care of her own needs and wants, not the wants of her adult mother. This child may learn how to give attention but never receive it, since she is always in the role of caregiver. Although the needs of the child remain strong, they are suppressed in favor of the needs of the parent. The child may become anxious, guilt-ridden, and isolated, since the parent's needs are always at the forefront of the child's mind. In adulthood, the daughter continues seeking relationships in which she can excessively caretake, leaving her own emotional needs unmet.

Tanya's Reluctance to Repeat

Tanya, a thirty-five-year-old married mother of five, sought out counseling after she began having panic attacks and anxiety. Tanya was a friendly and engaging patient. She quickly developed a therapeutic rapport and jumped into the work of uncovering the core of her anxiety.

Tanya was taking Lexapro for her panic attacks and, as a result, had gained about twenty pounds. Although she did not admit to being particularly distressed about the weight gain, she confided that her mother was very concerned about the weight gain and Tanya's health. Tanya also revealed that she was wearing braces because her mother had told her that she needed to "fix" her teeth and her bite; after all, she would "look so much more attractive." Her therapist asked her whether these were common interactions with her mother. She replied that they had been going on her entire life.

Tanya revealed that her mother controlled the entire household, including her father. Her mother was very preoccupied with how things looked on the outside and what other people might think about them. Tanya was aware of some of her mother's issues and knew she couldn't live up to her high standards. Now that she had children of her own, Tanya was worried that she was going to repeat some of the same behaviors her mother had exhibited.

Codependency and Narcissism

Codependency has long been associated with alcohol and drug addiction; however, narcissism and codependency are two sides of the same coin. Codependents and narcissists engage in a dance of dysfunction. Both are controlling, both can be manipulative, and both are boundaryless. However, codependency is an excessive dependence on another individual for a sense of self and identity. It develops as a result of focusing on another member of the family who is demanding all of the energy and attention. A child in a household with a narcissistic mother learns very early that adapting herself to the whims and fancies of her mother will produce a more positive outcome. The child's sense of worth is placed in the hands of her narcissistic mother, dependent on her mother's mood, frame of mind, and acceptance on that day. Narcissistic mothers demand all of their daughter's attention, relentlessly requiring them to move heaven and earth on a moment's notice but give nothing in return.

Daughters of narcissistic mothers learn a toxic definition of love. In this case, love means being responsible for the happiness of another person, when in reality, happiness is an individual responsibility.

Like narcissists, codependents' sense of self and self-importance comes from others. Unlike narcissists, codependents are empathetic, even overly empathetic, which makes them ripe for the controlling nature of narcissists. Recovering from the trauma of growing up with a narcissistic mother takes time. It starts with recognizing the toxic nature of the relationship with your mother and acknowledging that the messages and beliefs she delivered to you were untrue. Then you can discover how to meet your own needs.

Narcissism and Attachment Theory

Attachment refers to the bond between a parent and child that influences the child's ability to form healthy, mature relationships later in life. The theory of attachment originated with the work of psychiatrist John Bowlby and psychologist Mary Ainsworth. They suggested that children enter the world preprogrammed to form attachments with others. That is, a child desires security and closeness with their parents from birth. Children who feel safe with their parents are more likely to develop secure attachment styles. Children with unstable early experiences may have difficulty forming secure attachments later in life.

Being raised by a narcissist mother practically ensures that your attachment style will be insecure. A child whose needs are not met consistently does not learn to trust and will struggle with expressing emotions and dealing with feelings throughout her life. But there is good news. Attachment styles are not permanent, and with work, it's possible to overcome patterns learned in childhood.

In this next section, we'll examine the four attachment styles—secure, ambivalent (anxious), avoidant, and disoriented (disorganized)—and their relationship to the parenting of the maternal narcissist.

Secure Attachment

People with secure attachment are considered to be well-adjusted. Those with secure attachment have learned to depend on the people around them for support and emotional intimacy. Confident in their relationships, they can function independently while still meeting the needs of those around them. Narcissistic mothers fail to provide the love, care, and attention their child needs. This leads to an insecure attachment, which can be ambivalent, avoidant, or disoriented (we'll explore these next). Although a narcissistic mother may occasionally respond to her child's needs, the unpredictability creates anxiety, and the child is left believing their needs and desires are not important.

Ambivalent Attachment

Individuals with ambivalent attachment, sometimes referred to as anxious attachment, often struggle with overwhelming anxiety and fear that their loved one will abandon them. They seek constant reassurance and can be described as clingy. Narcissistic mothers do not consistently meet the needs of their daughters, confusing a child who is hardwired to attach to her parents. Although the narcissistic mother may meet the daughter's physical needs, the mother is unable to validate and reassure, so the child believes she is a burden. Because of a desperate need to connect to anyone, a person with ambivalent attachment may enter into relationships quickly and intensely, focusing only on a partner's interests and disregarding their own.

Avoidant Attachment

Avoidant attachment styles are the result of emotionally distant parents. When a narcissistic mother consistently leaves her child to their own devices, the child learns they must take care of their own needs and, as a result, may develop more adult-like behaviors. The child realizes they will not get their emotions met, so they block their desires for love, support, and bonding from others. Individuals with this attachment style are independent and don't want to rely on others for emotional closeness. People with avoidant attachment mask their fears by shutting people out.

Disoriented Attachment

Disoriented attachment, also known as disorganized attachment, is characterized by people who crave intimacy but also fear it. This style of attachment occurs when a child's only source of safety causes fear. It's the most difficult attachment problem to treat because it manifests characteristics of both avoidant and ambivalent attachment styles. When a narcissistic mother abuses (verbally, physically, or sexually), the child does not know what to expect and withdraws in fear, no longer trusting the mother. As adults, individuals with disoriented attachment expect and are always waiting for rejection. In their mind, it's inevitable.

Attachment Injury

A childhood attachment injury occurs when a child experiences a harmful event that affects the child's ability to bond with the caregiver or parent. It can occur as the result of abuse or neglect and can have a lasting effect on the ability to form healthy relationships. Disruptions in the bonding of daughters and their narcissistic mothers can lead to problems with trust and intimacy. A daughter who is unable to predict or rely on the consistent emotional support of her mother may grow to replay the role in her romantic relationships, acting on an unconscious desire to repair the relationship with her mother through her adult relationships.

UNDERSTANDING NARCISSISTIC SUPPLY

We know that narcissists derive their sense of self, validation, and admiration from others, so it stands to reason that they would collect these bits and pieces and hold on to them. Just as we need food to survive, a narcissist requires supply from their environment to survive. Narcissists are addicted to this supply and, as a result, spend endless energy attempting to acquire it.

There are many avenues whereby narcissists can gain their supply. Because supply is always external, their only option is to acquire it from outside themselves. They can secure supply through attention (approval, admiration, or affirmations), whether positive or negative. To a narcissist, achievements, whether real or imagined, are most important as long as they can get others to believe them. A narcissist is far more concerned with perception than with truth, and the narcissist's supply allows for a brief regulation of their volatile sense of self-worth.

When children are young, they are extensions of their mothers. Narcissistic mothers receive ample supply from their small children because children place their mothers on a pedestal. A child will do whatever their mother wants and will be compliant and controllable. As the child gets older and develops a mind of their own, supply begins to run low and the narcissistic mother feels threatened. This is when the narcissist digs into her arsenal, likely playing the victim, guilting, asserting parental authority, or sitting on a pity pot.

The Role of Enablers

For a narcissist or any manipulative person to continue taking advantage, there must be someone playing the enabler. An enabler is someone in the narcissist's life who encourages their destructive behavior. As a therapist, I see enabling behavior all the time. Enablers hide or clean up messes, apologize for the narcissist, blame others for the narcissist's behavior, and paint the narcissist as the victim. Enablers are often referred to as the "flying monkeys" of the narcissist, referring to the flying monkeys in *The Wizard of Oz*, who protected and carried out the plans of the Wicked Witch of the West.

Enablers can be a friend, family member, partner, child, or sibling. The enabler must be someone who is codependent and easily manipulated by the narcissist. These are generally the only people who remain in a narcissist's life for any period of time. People who have healthy boundaries and a solid sense of self would not tolerate the behaviors of a narcissist. This makes the child or daughter of a narcissistic mother especially prone to take on this role.

Identifying Enablers

How do you identify whether you enabled or have been enabling your mother? How do you identify others who enabled or may be enabling your mother? First, let's differentiate between someone who enables and someone who helps. Helping someone entails assisting and supporting a person who has every intention of improving their situation and is capable of doing so. Enablers try to solve or cover up problems for the narcissist, and an enabler will never hold the narcissist responsible for any abusive or inappropriate behaviors.

When trying to identify enabling behaviors in yourself or others around your mother, consider looking for the following indicators. Enablers will:

→ Tolerate or ignore problematic behavior

→ Cover up or make excuses for the narcissist's behavior

→ Avoid conflict to keep the peace

→ Do everything they can to protect the narcissist from feeling pain

→ Give the narcissist the benefit of the doubt over and over again

→ Shift the focus of the narcissist's behavior to the victim

The motivation for the enabler is to keep the peace and manage their own discomfort. A daughter of a narcissistic mother has convinced herself that she is the only person who can manage her mother's happiness. It is important to remember that you only enabled your mother because you had no other choice. As the child of a narcissistic mother, your job was to survive, and you did the best you could. You may have dismissed the actions of your mother because the risk of her withholding love and affection was too great for you to bear. Although this may be difficult, it's important to identify some of the enabling behaviors you may have engaged in so you can recognize them in the future. Some things daughters will say to excuse their mother include:

"She's like that with everybody."

"She's not very good at expressing her emotions."

"Nobody understands her."

"She doesn't mean the things she says."

"Don't take things so personally."

How Your Mother's Narcissism Affects You

When the bond between mother and daughter is damaged due to narcissism, the consequences for her daughter are significant. The daughter of a narcissistic mother may experience mental health and physical challenges. A narcissistic mother teaches her daughter that love is conditional and that relationships are dependent on her ability to make others happy.

Narcissistic abuse is considered trauma and can lead to post-traumatic stress. As a survivor, a daughter may feel as though she needs to be on constant alert. Survivors of narcissistic abuse live in a world of unpredictability and instability, and they're attracted to relationships and situations that mimic their childhood. They may have an overactive fight-or-flight response and experience hypervigilance, even when not in danger. As a result, a daughter may develop negative coping mechanisms, such as negative self-talk, substance abuse, or running away because she was never taught how to cope with life's ups and downs.

Lack of Self-Care

When we're sick or under stress, it can feel difficult or impossible to complete basic tasks of self-care. This is how a daughter of a narcissistic mother feels constantly. When our focus is always on another person, when we feel we can't ever please this person, when we expect negative feedback at any moment, the last thing we are thinking about is self-care. We're in survival mode. Since the daughter of a narcissistic mother is often isolated from friends or other support, she may have trouble realizing that she needs to help herself.

Self-Blame

Have you ever considered how many times a day you say "I'm sorry"? Many daughters of narcissistic mothers are shocked to find out how frequently they say it. They learn early on in life that they're going to have to take the blame for everything. Daughters of narcissists are told repeatedly that if they had done something differently, or had become a different person, then things could have been better. They believe they caused their mother to be mad, unhappy, or disappointed and that they were responsible for "making" her respond negatively.

Insecure Attachments

If a child does not have their emotional needs met by their caregiver, they will develop insecure attachment. This leads to an inability to feel safe and protected in any relationship. If you ask a person with secure attachment how they viewed their childhood, they may say they always felt able to rely on their caregivers. People with secure attachments are comfortable in intimate relationships and willing to take risks. Conversely, daughters of narcissistic mothers who develop insecure attachment styles will struggle with meaningful relationships throughout their life.

Complex Post-Traumatic Stress Disorder (CPTSD)

Many people are familiar with post-traumatic stress disorder (PTSD). PTSD is usually the result of exposure to a singular traumatic event, such as a car accident or a physical or sexual assault. These events can lead to flashbacks, nightmares, hypervigilance, and feelings of emotional detachment or numbness. Complex PTSD (CPTSD) is the result of repeated exposure to trauma and results in some PTSD symptoms, as well as a host of other issues. These issues can include problems with emotional regulation, dissociative symptoms (a feeling of detachment or being outside your body), and feelings of emptiness and hopelessness. A daughter of a narcissistic mother can experience all of these symptoms of CPTSD because she has been exposed to repeated trauma and abuse all of her life.

Mistrust of Others

An unreliable, untrustworthy mother who does not consistently meet the needs of her child is unable to instill a sense of trust in her child. In adulthood, this child's inability to trust others will manifest in their choosing emotionally unsafe people in their relationships. As humans, we are inherently attracted to familiar things and people. If you have been abused, it's likely you will be attracted to a person who may abuse you. You do it because that's all you know.

Self-Harming Tendencies

One of the most concerning effects of being abused by a narcissistic mother is the resulting risk of self-harm. Narcissistic mothers don't model how to appropriately manage emotions for their daughters. These daughters don't learn how to manage pain, conflict, or overwhelming emotions, so as adults they may resort to forms of self-harm to manage emotions. I have worked with women who have resorted to cutting, disordered eating, sexual promiscuity, and alcohol and drug abuse as a means of coping. Women who self-harm feel they are at fault and should punish themselves because their mothers were unable to love them or care for them.

Self-Gaslighting

Gaslighting is a form of emotional abuse that narcissists use to create doubt in the mind of their victims. The intention is to make the victim feel "crazy." A narcissistic mother will continually insist that their daughter's perceptions are wrong and inaccurate and that her daughter is the one with the problem. Hearing this over and over leads the daughter to internalize this "crazymaking" dialogue and use it on herself. Because she can't trust her own intuition, she may start to gaslight herself, using phrases like:

"Maybe it wasn't that bad."

"If I were stronger, I wouldn't feel this way."

"I should be over this by now."

"Why can't I just do the right thing?"

THE LONG-TERM EFFECTS OF EMOTIONAL ABUSE

In many ways, emotional abuse is an invisible disorder. Unlike physical abuse, emotional abuse leaves no visible clues to its presence. Many victims of emotional abuse hide in plain sight, never revealing the pain and anguish they have been through and still deal with.

Like abuse of any kind, the long-lasting effects can persist. Emotional abuse can contribute to low self-esteem, problems with self-identification, depression, anxiety, and chronic health problems. Survivors of emotional abuse have difficulty with trust and may have problems maintaining healthy relationships as adults. Emotional abuse can lead to PTSD or CPTSD, which manifests as negative thoughts, problems with emotional regulation, nightmares, hypervigilance, and dissociation.

Recognizing and accepting that you have experienced narcissistic abuse is the first step toward reclaiming your power. Often, people are not aware that they have been victimized. Growing up in a home with a narcissistic parent was your norm and may be difficult to understand. As you begin to come to terms with the reality of the abuse, you may decide to seek professional help to assist with processing your feelings and emotions. Seeking support and relief from any type of emotional abuse can be life-changing, but it is a journey, so it's important to have compassion and grace for yourself as you move through the process.

Key Takeaways

After working through chapter 2, I hope you're beginning to feel some validation and realize that you are not alone. As I frequently tell my clients, if someone has written a book about this issue, you are definitely not the only one who has experienced it. Realizing that you have survived narcissistic abuse is essential to healing. Having a parent who has repeatedly pointed out your deficiencies rather than your strengths can cause a negative narrative you may not be aware of. Give yourself permission to change that. The courage it takes to face the pain and abuse you have suffered is the definition of strength. This strength has been with you all along—you just needed to discover it!

Keep the following in mind:

→ Recovery from codependency includes discovering how to meet your own needs.

→ Bonding and attachment are learned, not innate, so it is possible to change your attachment style for the better.

→ Daughters are manipulated into enabling their mothers to acquire narcissistic supply.

→ The behaviors of a maternal narcissist are traumatic and can lead to PTSD or CPTSD.

PART TWO

RECOVERING FROM THE NARCISSISTIC MOTHER

Now that you understand your mother's behavior, let's take a deeper look at how your feelings were not validated or acknowledged. You might have feelings of inadequacy, sadness, and emotional emptiness. Part 2 of this book will help you identify and process emotions that you were unable to safely express as a child. Although you may find this work difficult at times, it will be worth it.

Daughters of narcissistic mothers sometimes wrestle with how to maintain an adult relationship with their mother. It is possible to develop skills that allow you to communicate with your mother in a healthy way. By establishing and setting firm boundaries, you will feel more comfortable interacting with everyone in your life, including your mother.

This work is also about breaking the cycle of abuse to ensure that you don't pass it on as well as gaining the tools to acquire and maintain emotionally connected relationships. Additionally, by recognizing the importance of self-care and its relationship to self-esteem, you can begin to cultivate the nurturing relationship with yourself that you deserve.

The chapters that follow will guide you through these steps for recovering from a narcissistic mother. Working on building your authentic self, learning how to manage the relationship with your mother in a healthy way, gaining tools to break the cycle of abuse, and learning to care for yourself are the skills that will help you move forward in your healing journey and, ultimately, feel fulfilled.

"When you feel at sea in an abyss of emotions, reconnecting to the beauty of your soul can be difficult, but it is never impossible."

—LORRAINE NILON

CHAPTER THREE

Processing Your Emotions

You may have discovered that dealing with narcissistic abuse in your childhood has impacted your entire life. Survivors of abuse often struggle with sadness, grief, and anger. You may feel that you live in survival mode. Survival mode means existing day to day while focusing on minimizing pain and suffering. These survival mechanisms have kept you from feeling powerless and defenseless.

All this said, your painful emotions have had a purpose. When you face and process these emotions, you experience feelings that you may have been suppressing for many years. But before you process your emotions, you need to understand them. This may be difficult, since you've been putting your mother's emotions before your own your entire life.

In this chapter, you will take the first steps toward your active recovery. You'll learn skills and build tools to acknowledge the damage caused by the relationship with your narcissistic mother. Exercises for getting to know your emotions can help you achieve a better understanding of how your emotions have affected your life. Practices and prompts will help you identify the trauma, thinking errors, and anger issues you may have overlooked. The process of recovery will help you rebuild your self-esteem, reconnect with yourself, and break free at last.

"Emotional susceptibility is the tendency to "catch" others' feelings (usually negative feelings), incorporate these feelings into yourself, and then find that you are unable to easily release them."

—NINA W. BROWN, EdD, LPC

Louise's Brave Realization

Louise came to therapy to help manage her anxiety. At twenty-six, she had just been named an administrator in her school system. She was married and had a two-year-old daughter. As far as everyone could tell, her life was perfect. But she felt like an impostor in her own life. Louise's parents divorced when she was a young child, and she had a complicated relationship with both of them. From a young age, her mother had criticized her, telling her that she wasn't a good daughter because she wouldn't always do the things her mother asked. Even now, her mother's unreasonable demands continued, such as telling Louise to let her adult brother live rent-free with her and to follow her mother's advice about raising her own daughter.

Things came to a head when Louise's mother criticized the decorations that Louise had chosen for her own daughter's party. Louise's mother told her that she was traumatizing her daughter. In telling this story, Louise realized that her mother had been doing this all along—criticizing her choices, making fun of her interests, and refusing to support her. This criticism had left Louise struggling to determine what made her happy in life. Louise had always believed there was something inherently wrong with her. Although she logically knew that her mother lacked some basic nurturing skills, she had never considered her mother a narcissist. Could this be the cause of her anxiety: spending her life trying to gain her mother's approval?

Louise realized that her mother's behavior toward her was abusive. Now she was ready to do the work of recovery to realize her self-worth as a daughter and a mother.

Easy Mindfulness Practice

It helps to remember that although you cannot change your past, you can learn how to relate to what has happened rather than react to it. Mindfulness allows us to relate differently to our experiences, both past and present. By learning to pay attention deliberately, we can learn how to remain present even when difficult emotions, thoughts, or sensations arise and threaten to shut us down.

Jon Kabat-Zinn, one of the first leaders in mindfulness, defines this practice as "paying attention in a particular way: on purpose, in the present moment, and nonjudgmentally." Try the following exercises to practice mindfulness.

- Pay attention to the experience of breathing: the sounds, rhythm, sensations, smells, and so on.

- Write with the opposite hand, text with your opposite hand, brush your hair with the opposite hand, or use a fork with your opposite hand.

- Intentionally choose to smile. Notice the immediate physiological response in your body. Smiling makes you "feel" good.

- Change your routine. Drive to work a different way, eat something different for breakfast, or reverse your morning routine. Be purposeful and thoughtful.

- Take a deep breath and hold it. Notice and name five things you can see, feel, hear, or smell.

> **I am putting the past behind me to focus on the present and future.**

Taking Inventory

One of the first things clients tell me when we meet are the issues that have brought them to my office. After growing up in an emotionally invalidating environment, you might have great difficulty understanding how your experiences have affected you. You may struggle to articulate how you feel. A good place to start is by taking an inventory of some of the internalized messages you may not even realize you've been repeating. The process of healing starts with identifying and understanding these negative messages. After all, you can't change messages if you don't know what they are.

Take a moment to review the following messages. Check the statements that resonate with you.

☐ I have difficulty trusting people.

☐ I struggle with intimate relationships.

☐ I worry I will become my mother.

☐ I believe I am emotionally immature.

☐ I have difficulty identifying and trusting my emotions.

☐ I feel empty inside.

☐ I have difficulty expressing myself.

☐ I worry about being a good mother.

☐ I feel uncomfortable around my mother.

You may have checked several statements or maybe just a few. If you experienced any anxiety or discomfort while reading through them, that's okay—you are learning to acknowledge them. You'll soon learn skills to effectively manage the uncomfortable emotions you feel.

Getting to Know Your Emotions

Now that you've taken inventory of your vulnerabilities, you can get to know your emotions. Emotions, thoughts, and behaviors are deeply connected, so it can be easy to confuse them. You might find it difficult to separate what you think from what you feel. For example, you may feel anxious and worry about failing at a new task, but it doesn't mean you will. Your emotions are just trying to warn you about potential threats.

Learning to manage your emotions starts with having a good grasp of what emotions are and how they affect your thoughts, your behaviors, and even your physical response. You may not have realized that emotions affect your body. When emotions are triggered in your brain, they send impulses to your body. By paying attention to your body, you'll be able to identify these physical changes.

Imagine each of the following emotions and how they tend to affect you. After reflecting, fill in the boxes, describing how each emotion affects your body, thoughts, and actions.

→

Getting to Know Your Emotions continued

EMOTION	BODILY RESPONSE (heart rate, body sensations, facial changes)	THOUGHTS (what you think about a situation)	BEHAVIORS (what you do when you feel the emotion)
FEAR			
ANGER			

EMOTION	BODILY RESPONSE (heart rate, body sensations, facial changes)	THOUGHTS (what you think about a situation)	BEHAVIORS (what you do when you feel the emotion)
SADNESS			
LOVE			

→

EMOTION	BODILY RESPONSE (heart rate, body sensations, facial changes)	THOUGHTS (what you think about a situation)	BEHAVIORS (what you do when you feel the emotion)
SHAME			
HAPPINESS			

Once you know how some emotions can affect you physically as well as cognitively and behaviorally, you may be able to identify and understand your emotions as you experience them.

My Feelings So Far

The work you have done so far is helping you not only with recovery but also with self-identity. As you begin to uncover and reveal how some of the abuse has affected you, you open a door to understanding yourself better. By identifying vulnerabilities and discovering how your emotions, thoughts, and behaviors connect, you begin to fill your toolbox of skills.

Set a timer for five minutes. Begin writing about what you have read in this workbook so far. What thoughts are you having about this subject? What does it feel like in your body?

_____

_____

_____

_____

_____

_____

_____

_____

_____

_____

_____

_____

_____

_____

How Am I?

The previous exercises and prompts may have brought out feelings that you didn't even realize you had. Checking in with yourself during the process of recovery is critical. As we've discussed, emotions affect your body and mind. As you are remembering, working on, and dealing with trauma, it is important to notice how you feel in your body and mind. Practice these steps for checking in with yourself.

1. Stop what you're doing.

2. Sit quietly for a short time.

3. Turn your attention inward and ask your body how it feels.

4. Notice tension anywhere in your body (shoulders, stomach, jaw, back).

5. Notice if you are holding your breath.

6. Notice if you are engaging in any behaviors that are the result of tension or anxiety (nail biting, skin picking, etc.).

7. Notice the emotions you feel. Do you recognize them (fear, sadness, anger, fatigue, loneliness)?

8. Are you able to stay focused, or do you have racing thoughts?

9. If you notice physical signs of tension or anxiety, use the breathing exercises described in "Four Square Breathing" (page 56) to self-soothe.

Self-Esteem Survey

Self-esteem is vital for leading a healthy life. Victims of abuse and trauma have issues with self-esteem. As we have explored, abuse and trauma affect whether we feel worthy or valued. Review the following statements, and rate how much you believe each statement on a scale of 0 to 5.

0 = almost never   **1** = rarely   **2** = sometimes
3 = frequently   **4** = most often   **5** = always

I am a good and worthwhile person.

0   1   2   3   4   5

I like being me.

0   1   2   3   4   5

When I look at myself in the mirror, I feel good about myself.

0   1   2   3   4   5

I am confident in my abilities.

0   1   2   3   4   5

I am comfortable expressing my feelings and emotions.

0   1   2   3   4   5

I am of equal value to others.

0   1   2   3   4   5

I am a good friend, partner, daughter, and neighbor.

0   1   2   3   4   5

→

I can handle difficult situations.

O   1   2   3   4   5

I like myself even when I'm dismissed by others.

O   1   2   3   4   5

I love myself no matter what happens.

O   1   2   3   4   5

If most of your responses fell in the O to 2 range, you may be struggling with your self-esteem. Low self-esteem can negatively impact many areas of your life, including relationships, careers, and, most importantly, your sense of well-being. The good news is, by assessing where your self-esteem falls, you can identify areas you may need to work on. As you move through this workbook, you'll learn how to develop problem-solving skills, assertive communication skills, and healthy boundaries, all of which will help you meet the potential you have always been destined to achieve.

A traumatic event can result in more than just awful memories. It can also spark reactions and problems that you might not recognize as trauma-related.

Circle the symptoms or issues you have had in the past or recognize now. **Underline** those you did not attribute to your trauma.

The process of recognizing symptoms of trauma can be intense, but acknowledging these symptoms can start breaking down avoidance. Write down the symptoms that have had the greatest impact on you.

_____

_____

_____

_____

Myths about Emotions

In this exercise, based on dialectical behavior therapy (DBT) developed by Marsha Linehan, we'll look at some myths about emotions. You may have learned some messages about emotions that you did not realize are myths. These may have contributed to you bottling up your emotions or not expressing them at all. Because your emotions were quieted and silenced, you may have some misconceptions about them that are worth exploring.

In this exercise, challenge yourself to write down a truth to contradict the following myths.

Myth: There is a right way to feel in every situation.

Truth: _____

Myth: Showing my emotions makes me weak.

Truth: _____

Myth: I should ignore painful emotions.

Truth: _____

Myth: Negative feelings are always bad.

Truth: _____

Myth: If other people don't agree with my emotions, then my emotions must be wrong.

Truth: _____

Myth: If I start crying, I will never stop.

Truth: _____

Myth: Emotions happen out of the blue.

Truth: _____

Dig Deeper

Processing emotions sometimes requires us to revisit painful memories so we can look back and identify what we were feeling. By this point, working through this workbook has probably stirred up memories and experiences you had with your mother. Although it may be difficult for you, consider this an opportunity to practice the strength and courage that have gotten you this far.

Think about an experience with your mother that caused painful emotions. What thoughts did you have about this experience? Identify negative emotions you had. What behaviors did you engage in as a result of the emotional pain? Were the behaviors helpful or unhelpful?

_____

_____

_____

_____

_____

_____

_____

_____

_____

_____

_____

_____

_____

_____

Four Square Breathing

Learning to regulate your breathing is one of the simplest ways to manage emotions. Anxiety and stress can cause you to take shallow, small breaths instead of deeper breaths through your diaphragm. Deep breathing is one of the best ways to manage stress. When you breathe deeply, your brain receives a message to calm down and relax. Almost immediately, the signs of being stressed (increased heart rate, fast breathing, elevated blood pressure) all decrease as you deeply breathe. This breathing exercise is a simple but effective way to regulate your breathing. You can practice this exercise at home, in the car, at your job, or even while you are speaking to your mother.

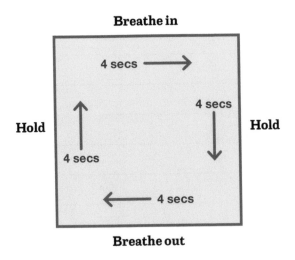

Here's how to do it:

1. Breathe in through your mouth for a count of four.

2. Hold your breath for a count of four.

3. Breathe out through your nose for a count of four.

4. Hold your breath for a count of four.

Repeat as many times as needed.

Thinking Errors

In this exercise, you'll consider how you look at yourself and the world. Trauma changes the way we view these things. This is normal, but sometimes we may get stuck in distorted thought patterns. These beliefs are known as faulty beliefs or thinking errors. Review the following thinking errors and check any that apply to you.

☐ **All-or-Nothing Thinking**
Looking at things in absolutes: all good or all bad; black and white.

☐ **Overestimating Harm**
Believing that harm is just around the corner; feeling that a one-in-a-million chance is the same as a 99 percent chance of something bad happening.

☐ **Perfectionism**
Feeling that you must do everything perfectly; otherwise it's intolerable.

☐ **Unrelenting Doubt**
Feeling that no matter what you do, you weren't careful enough, you've harmed someone, etc., so something bad will happen.

☐ **Magical Thinking**
Feeling that thoughts are so powerful, if you just think something bad will happen, it will.

☐ **Catastrophizing**
Believing it is always the worst-case scenario or that things are worse than they are.

☐ **Over-Responsibility**
Feeling that you must have caused something bad to happen and that if you failed at something, you must be a bad person.

☐ **Anxiety Intolerance**
Inability to tolerate feeling anxiety at all. You will do anything to feel better.

Checking off any of these boxes indicates that you have faulty beliefs or thinking errors that can be changed. Challenge your beliefs and replace them with positive self-talk to increase your coping skills.

Balancing Your Thoughts and Emotions

Now that you have a new understanding of your thoughts and emotions, it's time to learn to balance them. Survivors of narcissistic abuse often battle feelings of depression and anxiety that result from negative thoughts and self-talk. Victims of trauma often feel overwhelmed by their emotions because they only pay attention to part of what happened. To begin balancing your thoughts (and emotions), try to look at evidence that supports both sides of a thought.

Think of a recent distressing thought you have had. For example:

"I just can't do anything right."

"I feel like I will never enjoy my life."

"I'll never accomplish anything worthwhile."

Then answer the following questions to balance your thoughts.

What evidence supports your thought? What evidence is contrary to your thought?

_____

_____

_____

_____

Do you have evidence to support only bad things happening to you? Do you have evidence that good things happen, too? Write about both.

_____

_____

_____

_____

Do you have evidence that no one cares about you? Do you have evidence that people do care about you? Write about both.

_____

_____

_____

_____

What would a friend think about this situation? What do you think about this situation?

_____

_____

_____

_____

Getting to Know My Inner Child

Everyone has an inner child—an unconscious part of our mind that reflects our past. If you have experienced abuse or trauma, your inner child may have some healing to do. If the concept of the inner child is new to you, you may need to do some work to get to know her.

1. Find an old photo of yourself, from age eleven or younger. This photo should arouse feelings of protection, love, and vulnerability. If you don't have any pictures of yourself as a child, imagine yourself as a child.

2. As you look at/visualize your inner child, answer the following questions.

What age am I in the picture (or my visualization)? Why did I choose this age?

_____

_____

_____

What do I remember about this time in my life?

_____

_____

_____

What happened to me that hurt me during this time?

_____

_____

_____

How did my mother respond to my needs, feelings, or personality at this age?

_____

_____

_____

What were my hopes and dreams at this age?

_____

_____

_____

How did I change after this age?

_____

_____

_____

Dear Me

In my practice, I ask clients to write letters to themselves. Writing a letter to yourself helps you process what you've been through. It can also help you envision a path forward. When you translate your trauma into words, you begin to view your experience differently. It may be difficult to speak about what has happened to you, but writing it out may enable you to view your experience through another lens.

Write a letter to yourself. Permit yourself to name what you experienced at the hands of your narcissistic mother as abuse and trauma. An important element of moving forward and healing is admitting to yourself that you experienced abuse. Validate your feelings about the trauma, and include supportive words of comfort, support, and self-love.

_____

_____

_____

_____

_____

_____

_____

_____

_____

_____

_____

_____

_____

Thought-Stopping

Thought-stopping involves (1) focusing on unwanted thoughts and then (2) stopping and emptying the thoughts from your mind. Using the command "STOP" or visualizing a stop sign can interrupt unpleasant thoughts. Here's how:

1. Close your eyes and imagine a situation where an unpleasant thought is likely to occur. Think about how the negative or distressing thought relates to this situation.

2. Interrupt your thought.

   a. Set a timer for three minutes. Close your eyes and imagine the stressful thought. When the alarm goes off, shout "STOP!" and/or visualize a stop sign. Empty your mind of stressful thoughts. Try to allow your mind to stay empty for about thirty seconds. If the stressful thought returns, shout "STOP!" and visualize a stop sign again.

   b. Record yourself shouting "STOP!" Use the recording whenever you have distressing thoughts.

   c. When you have succeeded in extinguishing stressful thoughts by shouting "STOP," try interrupting thoughts with "stop" in your normal voice, and then start interrupting thoughts by whispering "stop." Once you're able to interrupt with a whisper, interrupt your thought by mouthing "stop." This will allow you to stop distressing thoughts in any environment without making a sound.

   d. Now, substitute the distressing thought with a positive, assertive statement. For example, if you're afraid to speak in front of a crowd, you might say to yourself, "I can do this; others want to hear what I have to say." Come up with several statements you can use to counter the negative statement.

Positive Self-Talk

Positive self-talk is one of the most effective ways to boost our self-esteem and change how we feel about ourselves. I always tell my clients, "Be your own cheerleader!" Positive and encouraging statements uplift and help with coping in distressing situations. Although it can sometimes be difficult, we can and should say supportive words to ourselves. You don't have to believe it to say it; you just need to say it to believe it. Over time, you will train your brain to believe the positive messages.

Examples of positive self-talk:

- *I am a worthy person.*

- *I am doing the best I can.*

- *I am not helpless. I can and will get through my recovery.*

- *My feelings are valid.*

- *One step at a time.*

- *I will be okay no matter what happens.*

- *I am a survivor.*

- *Feelings are not facts.*

Write down a positive statement for some difficult or distressing situations you encounter—something you can tell yourself that will help you get through. Type these statements on your phone, or take a picture to remind you.

DISTRESSING SITUATION	POSITIVE STATEMENT

Gratitude Journal

Gratitude is a powerful tool—it can change your entire outlook! At first, you may have a difficult time identifying things in your life to feel grateful for, but I assure you, there are plenty. No experience is too small to be grateful for. I'm hoping you'll use this exercise as a starting point in a long relationship with gratitude. Practicing gratitude can lead to more positive emotions, resiliency, and improvements in your health. It can also contribute to building positive relationships. Use the following prompts to start your gratitude journal.

Day 1

My favorite part of today was _____

_____

Something nice I saw someone do was _____

_____

Today I had fun _____

_____

Day 2

Today I accomplished _____

_____

Something funny that happened today was _____

_____

→

Gratitude Journal continued

I am thankful for _____

_____

Day 3

Today I was happy when _____

_____

Today was special because _____

_____

I was proud of myself today because _____

_____

Day 4

Something interesting that happened today was _____

_____

Something I smiled at today was _____

_____

I practice self-care by _____

_____

Day 5

Someone who inspired me today was _____

_____

Today I treated myself by _____

_____

Today I learned _____

_____

Don't end here—keep this thread going! Start a gratitude notebook, and jot down a few experiences with gratitude every day.

Alternative Message

Maternal narcissistic abuse chips away at self-esteem. The abuse you experienced damaged your spirit and changed the way you view yourself. Luckily, self-esteem can be rebuilt. Write down a word, phrase, or behavior that was used to chip away at your self-esteem. Next, describe how it made you feel about yourself. Then write a word, phrase, or behavior that counters that negative message. When you're finished writing, repeat your positive message out loud.

Quick Relaxation

There is a strong link between emotions and physical reactions. After a trauma, our bodies are in a heightened state of tension. Our bodies react to stress by contracting muscles, so muscle relaxation is a great way to reduce symptoms of stress and anxiety. It does so by sending calming messages to the brain. This helps us gain control over our emotions, but it takes practice. Practice this quick and easy muscle relaxation several times per week.

1. Tighten your fists, tighten your biceps and forearms, and then relax.

2. Wrinkle your forehead and roll your head in a complete circle clockwise. Reverse the roll. Then wrinkle your forehead, squint your eyes, push your tongue against the roof of your mouth, and shrug your shoulders up toward your ears. Then relax.

3. Arch your back and take a deep breath into your chest. Hold it for five seconds and release. Take another deep breath and push out your stomach. Hold it for five seconds, and then release.

4. Tighten your calf muscles, squeeze your thigh muscles, and flex your toes up toward you. Relax.

After you complete this exercise, notice how you are feeling. Are you more relaxed? Is there a noticeable difference in your body after the exercise?

> **I am a lovable, worthwhile person who deserves care and respect.**

Key Takeaways

After working through the exercises and activities in chapter 3, I hope that you are starting to understand how your mother's abuse affected you. Understanding your emotions, learning tools to manage them, recognizing trauma, and breaking away from unhealthy thinking patterns all help you work toward becoming a healthier version of yourself. As you move forward to the next chapter, remember all you have learned about your emotions, how they affect you, and the tools you can use to help you manage their intensity. It takes time and effort to work through and heal from the suffering caused by years of abuse. The ability to identify and process your complicated emotions is a skill you will value as you work toward healing.

Keep the following in mind:

→ Narcissistic mothers are unable to emotionally nurture, which leads to you internalizing negative messages about yourself.

→ Getting to know your emotions can help you understand how they affect your thoughts, your actions, and even your body so you can develop healthier patterns of coping.

→ Faulty beliefs and thinking errors that develop as a result of trauma can be identified and changed.

→ Recognizing your trauma and how it has affected you opens the door for self-soothing practices, including mindfulness, deep breathing, and journaling, which can help you work through and process difficult emotions.

→ Developing skills to balance your thoughts and emotions reduces negative thoughts and self-talk.

→ Getting to know your inner child helps you connect with the vulnerability and innocence you were deprived of so you can heal and begin to treat yourself with the understanding and compassion you deserve.

CHAPTER FOUR

Managing Your Relationship

In this chapter, we'll be exploring how to manage your relationship with your mother. Up until now, you have been working on exploring and identifying the emotions you have repressed for so long. This work has prepared you to better manage your relationship with your mother moving forward. This may seem like an impossible task, but there are a multitude of skills you can learn to better equip yourself to manage the mother-daughter dynamic.

Your relationship with your mother may be a roller coaster of thoughts, emotions, and behaviors, particularly when you try to interact with her. You will learn how to work on your relationships from a wise state of mind. This wise mind will set the stage for a balanced response to whatever your relationships may bring. As you practice this technique, you'll find you can better manage your emotions when triggers arise. By learning to establish and maintain boundaries, with your mother and in all your other relationships, you'll feel more in control of your own peace and contentment. You'll learn healthy communication skills that will assist you in asserting your boundaries and needs. Finally, you'll begin processing the grief of not having had the parent you should have had. This is a critical step in resolving old wounds so you can move forward.

"I was in denial of the glaring reality that my existence depended on my willingness to comply with the family policy of me earning the splinter of space granted to me."

—M. WAKEFIELD

Marta's Courage

Marta was struggling with whether to ask her mother to come stay with her after her breast cancer surgery to help with her kids. Her husband traveled for work, and her two children weren't old enough to drive or get themselves to their activities on their own. She needed the help but was hesitant to ask. She said her mother "drove her crazy," but she couldn't pinpoint exactly how. She dreaded the idea of her mother coming to her home.

Marta revealed that growing up with her mother had never been easy. Her parents divorced when Marta was a teenager, and she believed that her mother's controlling behavior pushed her father to leave. Her mother taught her to always be prepared for the worst because people were going to let her down.

Now, although her mother lived in another state, they talked every day. Their phone calls always seemed to focus on what her mother needed. Marta's mother never asked about her. Sure, she wanted to know details about things going on in Marta's life, but she never asked her how she was feeling. Now, Marta was in the most vulnerable place ever, and the one person whom she shouldn't hesitate to call was the last person she wanted. It wasn't that her mother wouldn't come; it was that her mother didn't listen. Her mother did what she wanted with seemingly no regard for anyone else.

Marta realized that she needed to establish boundaries with her mother. She needed to learn to assertively stand her ground and let her mother know what she needed when she needed it and what would happen if she didn't comply. Gradually, with the help of her therapist, she was able to set these boundaries with her mother, and eventually, her mother seemed to accept them.

Defuse Your Thoughts

During the process of recovery, it's not unusual to experience distressing thoughts. Sometimes you may get "stuck" on these thoughts. Learning to defuse or calm your thoughts is a technique borrowed from a methodology called acceptance and commitment therapy. Thought defusion enables you to see thoughts and feelings for what they actually are (streams of words or passing sensations), not what they declare they are (dangers or facts). This exercise teaches you how to take a step back from these thoughts and feelings. There are a few variations to try, so pick one or all to practice.

- Say your distressing thoughts or feelings very slowly out loud. Saying one syllable per breath is about the right speed. For example, if you're stuck on the thought "I'm unlovable," stretch it out and say "I'm," breathe in, say "un" on your breath out, say "love," breathe in, and then say "able" on your breath out.

- Say you are stuck on the following distressing thought: "I'm so worthless." Say this thought out loud. Now, say it as fast as you can. Say "I'm so worthless" over and over again. Try to say it faster and faster. Do it for 30 seconds.

- Another way to defuse your thought is to say your thought in a different voice. For example, if your thought is "I just can't do anything right," try saying it in a very high-pitched or low-pitched voice. You can use Mickey Mouse's voice or Homer Simpson's voice. Any voice you want to use will work.

The point with all of these defusing exercises is to realize that these are just thoughts and what you do with them is up to you.

> **I don't have to be perfect to be loved.**

Wise Mind

Before you begin working on managing your relationship with your mother, let's take a moment to examine how well you balance your emotional mind and your rational mind. This balance is known as the "wise mind." Having a wise mind helps you make sense of your thoughts and feelings so your responses to situations meet the needs of both your rational mind ("what I should do") and your emotional mind ("what I want to do").

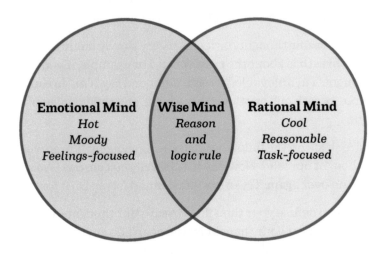

Describe an experience you've had with each of these states of mind:

EMOTIONAL	
RATIONAL	
WISE	

What steps can you take to practice wise mind responses with your mother?

"10 Things" Challenge

Working on the complicated topics of abuse and trauma can be emotionally demanding. Now that you are well into your work on your recovery, I hope you see just how strong you are. Take time to identify and write down ten things you have learned about yourself during your recovery process.

1. _____

   _____

2. _____

   _____

3. _____

   _____

4. _____

   _____

5. _____

   _____

6. _____

   _____

7. _____

   _____

8. _____

   _____

9. _____

   _____

10. _____

    _____

Identifying Emotional Triggers

You've learned about your emotions and understand why you feel the way you do. Now, take some time to look at things that activate those emotions. Triggers are cues or stimuli connected to traumatic events. They produce strong physical and emotional responses. As you move through your recovery, you may notice that certain things frequently trigger you. You can safely assume that whenever you are feeling overwhelmed, numb, or fearful, you have been triggered. Review the following triggers and check any that you have experienced.

- ☐ Loud or abrupt noises

- ☐ Certain smells

- ☐ Being touched

- ☐ Tone of voice

- ☐ Being ignored or dismissed

- ☐ Aggressive behavior

- ☐ Anniversaries, birthdays, or certain dates

- ☐ Reading or hearing specific words or phrases

- ☐ Being in a particular environment or place

By identifying what your triggers are, you can learn to anticipate and prepare for them in advance. This might allow you to take specific actions to reduce or respond to the effects.

Connecting Triggers

Let's take a deeper look at your triggers. We know that during your childhood, you didn't have an opportunity to focus on your emotions—your focus was on your mother. As a survivor of trauma, you remember trauma through your feelings and your body. You might notice that when certain situations occur, your emotional response does not fit the situation. If you can recognize when you're being triggered and how your body responds, this may help you identify your emotions and gain better control over your life.

To help you see the relationship between triggers and what happens to you when you get triggered (emotions or bodily responses), fill in the chart each time you are triggered. Write the date and time, and describe the situation (including intensity) in which you were triggered. Write in your reaction (thoughts, feelings, physical responses). Identify what happened just beforehand. How did you cope?

DETAIL THE SITUATION (including date, time, and intensity 1–10)	WHAT WERE YOUR FEELINGS, THOUGHTS, AND PHYSICAL SENSATIONS?	WHAT HAPPENED JUST BEFOREHAND?	WHAT DID YOU DO TO COPE?

Radical Acceptance

While doing this work, you may notice painful emotions revealing themselves. Radical acceptance involves learning to accept things completely and without judgment. Becoming skilled at radical acceptance takes practice, but it's a pivotal skill for recovery. Radical acceptance requires you to:

Observe whether you are fighting or doubting reality. Let go of "should haves," "would haves," and "could haves."

Remind yourself that you cannot change the past or predict the future. You only have the current moment.

Practice using a mantra for acceptance of the situation; for example, "it is what it is" or "so be it." Repeat this mantra to release the desire to control things when you feel distressed.

Look at events from a nonjudgmental viewpoint. Try not to place labels ("good" or "bad") on people, thoughts, and objects. Judgments can trigger overwhelming emotions.

Forgive yourself for mistakes you make. Use them as learning experiences rather than reasons to beat yourself up.

Plan how you will cope ahead of time with events that are difficult to accept. Rehearse in your mind what you might do to accept what happens. *Example:* Your mother has asked to visit you because she wants to give you a gift. The idea of a visit from her increases your anxiety and stress levels. Coping ahead might include writing down how you want to respond to her, practicing self-affirmations, or accepting that you cannot control her responses or reactions, only your own.

Allow yourself to feel disappointment, sadness, or grief without judgment.

Acknowledge that you can live life even when there is pain.

What Are Boundaries?

Wouldn't it be nice to be able to emotionally protect yourself when you are communicating with your mother? It would be life-changing! To do that, you must learn to set limits on what you will accept from her. Of course, she won't like the limits you set and may fight them; after all, she is used to being the one in control.

Before we can set these limits, or boundaries, we need to understand exactly what they are. Boundaries are physical, emotional, and mental limits we set to protect ourselves. Boundaries provide a guideline for healthy relationships with others. Your personal boundaries teach other people (including your mother) how to treat you.

The goal is to learn healthy boundaries. A person with healthy boundaries can be vulnerable but can also say "no." Review the common traits of each type of boundary, and check the ones you relate to.

RIGID	ENMESHED	HEALTHY
☐ Has few close relationships	☐ Is easily influenced by others' opinions	☐ Values own opinion
☐ Has difficulty asking for help	☐ Is overinvolved in others' problems	☐ Can say "no" without guilt
☐ Keeps people at a distance	☐ Fears rejection	☐ Appropriately shares personal information
☐ Avoids intimacy	☐ Feels responsible for others' emotions	☐ Doesn't compromise values
☐ Seems detached	☐ Struggles saying "no"	☐ Is able to communicate wants and needs
☐ Doesn't share personal information	☐ Overshares personal information	

If most of your checks fall into the rigid or enmeshed categories, don't despair. Right now you're just learning about what boundaries you do or don't have. As you move forward, you'll learn exactly how to put healthy boundaries into place.

Types of Boundaries

Now that you have a better idea about whether your boundaries are healthy, rigid, or enmeshed, let's look at the different types of boundaries. This knowledge will help you recognize if your boundary is being violated.

Physical boundaries include personal space and physical touch. People have different perspectives on what they consider appropriate physical touch. These boundaries can be violated if someone touches you more than you want or if someone invades your personal space.

Emotional boundaries refer to your feelings. With healthy emotional boundaries, you place limitations on how quickly you share personal information and with whom. This allows a relationship to develop gradually. Emotional boundaries are violated if someone belittles, criticizes, or invalidates your feelings.

Intellectual boundaries include your thoughts and ideas. Healthy intellectual boundaries are respectful of others' ideas and thoughts and allow everyone to express an opinion. A parent having an inappropriate conversation with a child is violating that child's intellectual boundary.

Material boundaries refer to your possessions. You can decide if you want to share your possessions with others, but with an expectation that the possessions will come back in the same condition. These boundaries can be violated if someone pressures you to lend or give them your possessions.

Time boundaries refer to how you manage your time. They include how well you manage work-life balance, self-care, and prioritizing your needs. These boundaries are violated when someone demands too much of your time.

In the following chart, identify a boundary in each category that you would like to set for yourself.

PHYSICAL

EMOTIONAL

INTELLECTUAL

MATERIAL

TIME

Boundary Maintenance

As a child, you were likely not taught about healthy boundaries, so you probably "made it up" as you went along. That's okay; you're in the right place now. There are two important things to remember to be successful with your boundaries. First, you have to be consistent with them so people know you mean what you say. Second, you must communicate a consequence for any boundary violation.

This exercise may feel uncomfortable at first, but it's one of the most important skills you can have in your relationships. Choose a boundary that you wish to set with your mother (or anyone else). In the first column, identify what boundary you want to set. In the second column, write exactly how you plan to explain it. Be clear and direct about what you need. In the final column, write why this boundary is important to you and what will happen if it is violated.

DEFINE	COMMUNICATE	SET CONSEQUENCES
Identify your boundary.	Clearly and simply state what you need.	Say why it's important.
Example: *Your mother criticizes your job.*	Example: *"I would like to talk with you about my job, but I would like you to avoid criticizing my choices."*	Example: *"It is important for me to feel like I can share things about my job without being criticized. If you cannot respect this, I won't talk about my job with you in the future."*

Boundaries, Boundaries, Boundaries

Boundaries are learned. Our parents teach us, for better or worse, what boundaries look like. Let's explore what boundaries looked like in your home. What were some boundaries that you learned growing up? What boundaries do you think would have been helpful? Did you feel safe setting boundaries with your family?

_____

_____

_____

_____

_____

_____

_____

_____

_____

_____

_____

_____

_____

_____

_____

_____

_____

_____

Grounding

As you work through these exercises, you may experience unwanted memories and negative emotions that make you feel unsafe or fearful. Grounding is a practice you can use to distract yourself from what you are experiencing and help you focus on what's happening in the present moment. Grounding is not a relaxation skill, but rather a tool to help you detach from difficult emotions. Most grounding techniques involve some aspect of your five senses (taste, touch, sight, smell, or hearing). Here are some grounding strategies to get you started.

- Press your feet firmly on the ground. This will remind you of where you are.

- Rub your hands together rapidly. Notice the sound and feeling of your hands.

- Carry a silky piece of cloth or a smooth stone with you to touch.

- Find your pulse on your wrist or neck and count the beats per minute.

- Reach your arms and hands to the sky. Stretch like this for five seconds. Bring your arms down and relax them at your sides.

- Slowly and deliberately cross your arms and legs. Feel the sensations of you controlling your body.

- Notice the smells in the air around you (air freshener, mowed grass, etc.). Find something with a scent, such as a candle, flower, or canister of coffee.

What's Your Communication Style?

Now that you know some ways to protect yourself through boundaries, let's work on communication. Communication can always be improved upon, but first let's look at the different types of communication and the style you tend to use most often. Review the different styles of communication, and check the statements you are most familiar with.

Passive

☐ Other people will get angry or ignore me if I express my feelings.

☐ I try to keep quiet because I don't want to upset anyone.

☐ I'm more comfortable ignoring my feelings than communicating them.

☐ I don't express myself when something matters to me.

☐ I usually go along with other people's opinions to avoid conflict.

Aggressive

☐ I can be intimidating at times.

☐ I always put my own needs and goals first regardless of others around me.

☐ It's my way or the highway.

☐ I swear, yell, and am verbally aggressive with people.

☐ I don't care if the needs of the people around me are met.

Passive-Aggressive

☐ I can be sarcastic when I feel angry.

☐ I agree to do things other people want me to do, even when I don't want to.

☐ When I'm angry, I give the silent treatment.

☐ I procrastinate or make intentional mistakes rather than expressing my emotions clearly.

☐ I complain about feeling misunderstood or unappreciated.

→

Assertive

- ☐ I actively listen and reflect back to other people so they know I hear them.

- ☐ I state my thoughts and feelings about situations, and I am good at compromising.

- ☐ I explore solutions, brainstorm, and ask for more information if I need it to make decisions.

- ☐ I take accountability for my mistakes.

- ☐ I am respectful to myself and others when I communicate.

If most of your selections fell in the passive, aggressive, or passive-aggressive categories, you may need to strengthen your assertive communication style. In the next exercise, you'll learn how to adjust your communication style to get what you want.

Effective communication skills are key to interacting, especially with a narcissistic mother. Learning to assert your needs while getting along with others is key to a healthy relationship. Dialectical behavior therapy (DBT) involves learning skills that can help you get what you want. The following DBT skill uses the acronym DEAR MAN to help you assertively communicate with your mother.

Describe. Describe the situation objectively. Stick to the facts; avoid opinion and explanation. The goal is to get everyone on the same page. *Example:* "You told me you would come to my appointment with me, but you didn't tell me you couldn't make it."

Express. Let your mother know how a situation makes you feel by clearly expressing your feelings. Don't expect her to read your mind. Try using "I feel" or "I want" statements. *Example:* "When you don't let me know you can't make it, I feel worried about you."

Assert. ASK for what you want or say NO clearly. Don't beat around the bush. Stand up for yourself. *Example:* "I would really like it if you would let me know when you can't make it."

Reinforce. Reward your mother by explaining the positive outcome. If necessary, clarify the negative outcome of not getting what you want or need. *Example:* "When you communicate with me, I'll want to include you in more activities."

(Be) **Mindful.** Keep focused. Don't get distracted. Repeat your message over and over. Ignore attacks; don't respond to threats or attempts to divert you.

Appear confident. Maintain good eye contact, posture, tone, and body language.

Negotiate. Be willing to compromise and negotiate. Offer solutions focused on what will work for both of you.

Now, choose a specific interpersonal challenge you are dealing with or have dealt with in the past. Answer the following prompts to create a plan for communicating assertively.

→

DESCRIBE	What are the facts of the situation?
EXPRESS	Write an "I" statement to express your feelings.
ASSERT	How will you tell your mother what you need? What specific language will you use?
REINFORCE	How will you reward your mother for responding positively to you?
(BE) MINDFUL	What is your goal? What things might distract you from this goal?
APPEAR CONFIDENT	Describe the posture, eye contact, and tone of voice you will use.
NEGOTIATE	What are you willing to give to get?

Reflecting on Boundaries

Setting boundaries for the first time with someone—especially your mother—can feel scary and overwhelming. These are normal feelings. To gain the courage and strength to practice your boundaries, consider your thoughts and feelings about setting boundaries with your mother. What are you fearful of? What might make you anxious? List any feelings you have about setting these boundaries. Write some affirmations that might help you stick to your boundaries.

_____

_____

_____

_____

_____

_____

_____

_____

_____

_____

_____

_____

_____

_____

_____

_____

_____

_____

Visualization

Imagery is one of the most effective ways to quiet the mind. Visualization involves deliberately using imagery to relax your body and change the way you feel and behave. Choose a quiet environment where you can be free from distractions. Get into a comfortable position, and give yourself time to relax before you start. You can use the mindfulness or quick relaxation practices outlined in chapter 3 (page 43 or 69). As an example, we will use a beach for visualization, but you can choose any visualization you like.

Visualize a beach in your mind. Imagine every detail.

Sight: *You're surrounded by white sand, and the sun is high above you. The water is emerald green, and the ocean waves are gently rolling in and out.*

Sound: *You can hear the pounding and swishing of the waves crashing onshore. Seagulls are calling from the sky.*

Smell: *The ocean air is fresh and salty. You smell faint whiffs of seaweed.*

Touch: *The sun is warm on your body. You feel sand between your toes and the ocean spray on your face. There is a warm, gentle breeze blowing.*

Taste: *You have a tall, cold glass of lemonade. It's tart, tangy, and sweet.*

Letting Go

Letting go is a decision to free yourself from the expectations of others so you can be the person you're supposed to be. Having a narcissistic mother blocked you from being free to be yourself or experiencing things in life that make you happy. Now that you're well on your way to recovery, let's identify some obstacles that might be preventing you from fully letting go of others' expectations. In this exercise, identify obstacles to let go of, and reflect on what the result might be.

Irrational beliefs:

Example: I will never be happy again.

_____

If I let go (of this belief):

_____

Fear of rejection or loss of approval:
Example: Others will not accept me for who I am.

_____

If I let go (of this fear):

_____

Fear of the unknown:
Example: I always have to know what will happen.

_____

If I let go (of this need):

_____

Letting Go continued

Avoidance of guilt:
Example: Others may blame me for their problems.

_____

If I let go (of guilt):

_____

Fear of conflict:
Example: Others will be angry with me.

_____

If I let go (of this fear):

_____

Fear of being disloyal or unfaithful:
Example: I must protect you no matter what, so I can't let go.

_____

If I let go (of this responsibility):

_____

Grieving the Relationship

Most of us have experienced some type of loss in our lives. In some cases, perhaps you didn't realize at the time that you grieved the loss. Grief plays a significant role in your relationship with your narcissistic mother. Grieving the loss of the mother you didn't have and you deserved may be one of the hardest things you do in your recovery. It is necessary to process this grief, however, to move forward.

Answer the following questions.

What does grief feel like to you?

_____

_____

_____

_____

In what parts of your body do you feel grief?

_____

_____

_____

_____

When do you feel the grief? How do you respond when you feel it?

_____

_____

_____

_____

$\rightarrow$

Grieving the Relationship continued

How can your grief work for you instead of against you?

_____

_____

_____

_____

Letter to Your Inner Child

Remember the exercise "Getting to Know My Inner Child" from page 60? Let's take it a step further. Write a letter to the abused child you once were. Imagine you are now your inner child's mother. Include supportive statements you wish you had heard from your mother. Keep this loving message with you, or record it so you can refer to it when you're feeling overwhelmed or sad.

_____

_____

_____

_____

_____

_____

_____

_____

_____

_____

_____

_____

_____

_____

_____

_____

_____

_____

_____

Most of the focus so far has been about the negative experiences you've had in your life. Let's take some time to think about things that excite and motivate you. During the day, set three timers to alert you to stop and think about something that excites you and something that motivates you. This can be anything from the cup of coffee you're drinking to the trip you'll be taking this summer. During these moments, practice being present with your thoughts. Refrain from judgment about what you are thinking about.

> **My feelings and needs are important.**

Key Takeaways

After working through the exercises and activities in chapter 4, you may have decided to make some difficult decisions. I commend you! Learning to establish boundaries, improve communication, and ask for what you want takes a great deal of courage. This journey isn't easy, but it will be worth it in the end. The skills you've learned in this chapter will benefit you in all of your relationships moving forward, including with your mother. Learning to advocate for yourself takes practice, but it's a skill that will help you respect yourself and make you feel satisfied. As you continue, remember these skills and abilities you now possess.

Keep the following in mind:

→ A wise mind helps you balance the way you express yourself.

→ By understanding your triggers, you can better manage your emotional responses.

→ As you work to establish healthy boundaries, remember that you are protecting yourself and your rights.

→ Assertive communication allows you to assert your needs and get what you want while being respectful of others' rights, too.

→ The process of grieving can help you move forward in your recovery.

CHAPTER FIVE

Breaking the Cycle

Breaking the cycle of abuse can feel like a formidable task. You may fear that being raised by a narcissist guarantees that you will think and behave in the same ways. Rest assured, this chapter will help you explore how to break the toxic cycle of hurt and abuse. In order to ensure that the cycle of abuse stops with you, there are several things you must examine.

The first is your family story. Narcissistic abuse did not start with you or your mother. There was likely some dysfunction that extended beyond your family of origin. When you consider this dysfunction now, the purpose is not to blame anyone, but rather to give you a better view of your story. Knowing your family story involves exploring your past and present so you can successfully end the cycle of abuse.

Knowing your story is just the first part. As with most children who have experienced abuse, you likely did not learn what healthy relationships looked like. As you come to recognize qualities you want others to have in your relationships, you'll empower yourself to break the cycle of dysfunction. In this chapter, you'll continue to assess and work on your self-esteem, values, and sense of self with exercises that focus on strengthening your view of yourself. Finally, you will create a mantra for yourself and a code of well-being to live by, which will help you build on your amazing resilience as you move forward in your life.

"You can recognize survivors of abuse by their courage. When silence is so very inviting, they step forward and share their truth so others know they aren't alone."

—JEANNE MCELVANEY

Kayla's Codependency Conundrum

Kayla is a forty-two-year-old single woman who sought counseling for codependency. Kayla had done a lot of her own research on ways to curtail her enabling behaviors. She attended Codependents Anonymous for many years and read nearly every self-help book available.

She had been married several times—the first time when she was seventeen. She married the first boy who showed her affection and what she considered love. Kayla had not received much of either from mother, who was always "absorbed with her own problems." Kayla explained. She could never rely on her mother for anything growing up. Kayla often wondered what she could do to gain her mother's attention and love. It seemed that nothing worked. Kayla's father didn't have much attention to give, either.

Kayla knew her mother's behavior was dysfunctional, but she felt trapped and helpless as a child. She tried very hard to break the cycle of abuse with her own children. Her eldest children lived with their dad, but she continued to raise her youngest daughter, whose father was out of the picture. Kayla was worried that she was continuing the cycle of abuse with her youngest daughter. She knew there were times when she wasn't the best mother, fluctuating between yelling at her daughter and ignoring her.

Kayla wanted to learn the tools to make sure her daughter grew up in a healthy home. Kayla committed herself to learning about healthy relationships, working on her self-esteem and values, and rebuilding her sense of identity. In her final session, Kayla's daughter accompanied her mother to talk about how much things improved recently. Kayla appreciated her daughter's words and support. Although Kayla knew she still had work to do, she promised her daughter that she would continue to work toward a healthy, supportive relationship.

Loving-Kindness Meditation

Showing compassion for yourself after abuse takes practice, but you can learn how to arouse long-suppressed feelings of self-compassion. A loving-kindness meditation invites you to focus kind and loving energy on yourself. There are many benefits, including increasing positive emotions, activating empathy, and reducing self-criticism. Here's how:

1. Sit in a comfortable position and relax.

2. Take two or three deep breaths with slow, long exhalations.

3. Let go of any concerns or distractions.

4. For a few minutes, feel or imagine your breath moving through the center of your chest into the area of your heart.

5. Sitting quietly, repeat, slowly and steadily, the following or similar phrases:

   - *May I be happy.*

   - *May I be well.*

   - *May I be safe.*

   - *May I be peaceful and at ease.*

6. While you say these phrases, allow yourself to sink into the intentions they express.

Sometimes during a loving-kindness meditation, you may feel anger, grief, or sadness. View these negative feelings as signs of progress, indicating that you are now able and willing to release them. Notice them leave you with your exhalations.

> **I accept all the different parts of myself.**

My Family Story

We've touched on how dysfunction in families can be passed down from one generation to the next. The impact of narcissistic trauma on a family can be complicated. Family members frequently play different dysfunctional roles in a family with narcissistic abuse. As a child of a narcissist, you may gravitate to people who remind you of this dysfunction. Understanding your family's trauma and how it affected you can be extremely helpful in understanding yourself from a different viewpoint. Respond to each question as honestly as possible.

Describe each of your family members with two or three adjectives (parents, caretakers, grandparents, siblings, children).

_____

_____

_____

_____

_____

_____

_____

Briefly describe your parents' (or caretakers') and grandparents' marriages.

_____

_____

_____

_____

_____

_____

Were there traumatic issues or losses within your family? These could be addictions, infidelities, sudden deaths, chronic illnesses, miscarriages, bankruptcy, abuse, divorce, depression, mental illness, and so on.

_____

_____

_____

_____

_____

_____

How did your family talk about feelings?

_____

_____

_____

_____

_____

_____

→

My Family Story continued

Were there any family "secrets" (such as pregnancy out of wedlock, incest, a major financial scandal, etc.)?

_____

_____

_____

_____

_____

_____

How do you think your family's background shaped you?

_____

_____

_____

_____

_____

_____

Understanding Family Drama

The "drama triangle" is a theory of dysfunctional family role-playing created by psychologist Stephen Karpman. In the drama triangle, each point represents a dysfunctional reaction to a situation. Family members create drama for themselves and others in these roles. Family members may jump from role to role during a conflict. You may find these roles familiar to you and your family dynamics. Understanding your family dynamic will help you develop new solutions to family conflict.

Victims are helpless, adopt a "poor me" attitude, and blame others.

Rescuers are enablers; they avoid true feelings and neglect their own needs.

Persecutors abuse others and use guilt to control. They blame the victim and criticize the enabling behaviors of the rescuers.

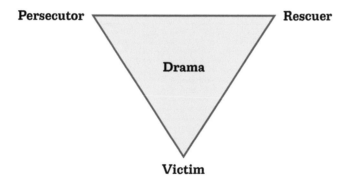

Consider the roles that were played in your family.

Victim: Write about a time in which you felt helpless.

_____

_____

_____

$\rightarrow$

Understanding Family Drama continued

Rescuer: Give an example of a time when you rescued someone from their consequences, even though you were trying to help.

_____

_____

_____

Persecutor: Write about a time in which you were critical or accusatory.

_____

_____

_____

Finding Empowerment

Now that you have a better understanding of the dramatic roles in your family system, let's discover how to develop healthier family roles. The opposite of the drama triangle is the "winner's triangle," developed by counselor Acey Choy. In the winner's triangle, each person takes responsibility for their role, their behaviors, and their feelings.

Problem-solvers are vulnerable and self-aware.

Caregivers do not do more than their share, do not problem-solve for others, and do not do things they don't want to do.

Asserters ask for what they want, can say "no," give feedback, and don't punish or put down.

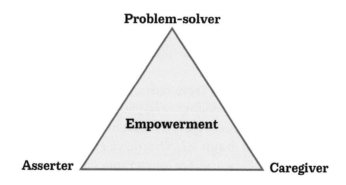

Problem-solver: Review the example from the previous exercise, in which you were the victim. What did you actually want? Try to think of a solution to the problem.

_____

_____

_____

→

Caregiver: Review the example in the previous exercise in which you rescued some-one. In what ways can you listen without trying to solve another person's problems?

_____

_____

Asserter: Review the example in the previous exercise in which you were critical. What did you miss in your communication that might have led to this outcome?

_____

_____

Resiliency

Resiliency is the ability to recover from setbacks and adapt to change. The work you're doing in this book has no doubt tested your resiliency. What factors have helped you work on your recovery from emotional abuse? What do you think feeds your resiliency? What drains it? What do you think defines a strong person? Would you identify yourself as a strong person?

_____

_____

_____

_____

4 5 6 Self-Compassion Pause

Self-compassion is the cornerstone of recovery and can improve many areas of your life, including your health, mood, and self-confidence. The relationship you develop with yourself is more important than anything. Without self-love, we can't reach our full potential. This mindfulness-based practice will help you learn to pause when you are experiencing overwhelming or challenging emotions. It includes a focused relaxing phrase that you'll use while you are calmly breathing. Use any soothing phrase you like—this phrase will help you return to a loving place of support.

1. Close your eyes.

2. Breathe in through your nose for a count of **4**.

3. Repeat to yourself, *"I have done my best."*

4. Hold your breath for a count of **5**.

5. Breathe out for a count of **6**.

6. Repeat to yourself, *"Now, let go of the rest."*

Repeat two or three times.

Healthy Relationships 101

Healthy relationships are supportive and respectful. They allow for opportunities for positive experiences, which, in turn, affect self-esteem. It takes time and care to create a healthy relationship, and the first step is to consider basic traits of healthy relationships. There are many elements of a healthy relationship that daughters of narcissistic mothers were never taught. In this exercise, you'll examine words that correlate with a healthy relationship.

Review the following words, and check the five traits you believe to be most important in healthy relationships.

☐ Trusting   ☐ Accepting

☐ Honest   ☐ Positive

☐ Compromising   ☐ Compassionate

☐ Supportive   ☐ Empathetic

☐ Reliable   ☐ Forgiving

☐ Encouraging   ☐ Safe

☐ Open and communicative   ☐ Equitable

Reflect on why you feel the traits you chose are so important for a healthy relationship.

_____

_____

_____

_____

_____

Note: There are no wrong answers in this exercise. Whatever healthy traits you chose as most important clearly matter to you and can serve as a template for what to look for in relationships.

Qualities I Want in Relationships

Now you have an idea of what traits are important to you in a healthy relationship. This is good because breaking the cycle of abuse also means beginning to discover what qualities you want in your relationships. Whether with friends, family, coworkers, romantic partners, or your own children, it's important to consider what you want to bring to the relationship as well as what you want others to bring. Check the qualities that are most important in your relationships.

☐ Compassion

☐ Consideration

☐ Maturity

☐ Dependability

☐ Trustworthiness

☐ Generosity

☐ Humor

☐ Self-discipline

☐ Diligence

☐ Patience

☐ Confidence

☐ Assertiveness

☐ Respect for self and others

☐ Integrity

Think about the relationships you currently have. Do you think you're in relationships with people who possess the qualities you checked? Do you think you bring these things to your current relationships?

_____

_____

_____

_____

_____

_____

_____

→

Qualities I Want in Relationships continued

What obstacles may have kept you from forming healthy relationships?

_____

_____

_____

_____

_____

_____

_____

_____

What would you like to change or adapt about yourself that can help you improve your relationships?

_____

_____

_____

_____

_____

_____

_____

_____

Challenging My Inner Critic

Daughters of narcissistic mothers have no shortage of negative thoughts and emotions. Our inner critic is always with us and can be useful at times, but when our critic is louder than it should be, we need to take action. On the lines, list every negative statement you can think of that you tell yourself; try to remember every self-critical and damaging message you have repeated over and over in your head. Take your time. When you have completed your list, write a second list with positive self-affirming statements to counteract each negative statement.

_____

_____

_____

_____

_____

_____

_____

_____

_____

_____

_____

_____

_____

_____

_____

Self-Regulation Practice

Working through the exercises in this workbook, or just everyday life, may result in feelings of distress, anxiety, or overwhelm. Trauma activates the central nervous system, which can leave you feeling chronically anxious, restless, and irritable. Self-regulation can help you calm your nervous system. If you have felt on high alert or are dealing with stressful events, working with your physical senses may help you feel better.

Try these two easy techniques to practice self-regulating:

- Hug yourself. Cross your right arm over your chest, placing your hand on your left shoulder. Then cross your left arm, placing your left hand on your right shoulder and squeeze gently. This practice can help you feel safe and accepted. Hold the hug for as long as you need.

- With your hand in a cupped position, tap your body all over, from your feet to your head. You can also try constricting different parts of your body instead of tapping them. This will help you with grounding, which you practiced on page 84. It can also help your body recognize your boundaries. You will begin to realize your ability to create your own safety and security.

Committing to Esteem and Confidence

On page 51, you completed an exercise to assess your self-esteem. Regardless of whether your assessment was more positive or negative, working on self-esteem is a lifelong endeavor. It's also an active process that requires you to look at your behaviors, thoughts, and feelings to promote growth and change. To break the cycle of narcissistic abuse, you'll want to practice and assess your self-confidence regularly so you can make changes wherever needed.

In the following table, review and answer the questions about each situation.

SITUATION	DESCRIBE THE SITUATION	WHAT WAS YOUR SELF-TALK? What did you tell yourself about the situation?	HOW DID YOU FEEL PHYSICALLY? What feelings and sensations did you have?	WHAT ACTION DID YOU TAKE?
You felt confident, satisfied, and worthy.				
You felt a lack of confidence.				

Committing to Esteem and Confidence continued

Review your answers about the situation in which you experienced a lack of self-confidence. Answer the following questions.

What positive affirmation could I say to myself to remind me of my strength?

_____

_____

_____

_____

What could I do that would help me feel differently?

_____

_____

_____

_____

What could I do differently the next time I am in this situation? What actions would empower me?

_____

_____

_____

_____

Feel free to recreate this chart and complete it regularly to gauge your self-confidence and reflect on ways to respond in the future.

Exploring Values

So much of your identity has been wrapped up in your mother's view and perception of you. To figure out how to break the cycle of abuse, you must work to figure out yourself. Exploring your values is a helpful way to realize who you are at your core. Values are the beliefs and principles of everyday living that are important to you. Everyone has different values, so there are no "right" or "wrong" answers.

Review the list of values in the first column, and rate how important each one is to you by writing 1 (not important) to 4 (very important) next to it. In the next column, explain why this value is at the level of importance that you rated it. At the bottom, feel free to add other values that resonate with you.

RANKED VALUES	WHY IS THIS VALUE IMPORTANT TO YOU?
Family relationships	
Intimate relationships	
Friendships/social relationships	
Work/career/education	
Spirituality	
Recreation/relaxation	
Helping others (people/animals/causes)	
Physical health	
Other: _____	
Other: _____	
Other: _____	

Transform Values into Action

When you were growing up, your values were likely dictated by your narcissistic mother. Now that you've identified values that are important to you (page 115), look back on some of the values you selected. Consider whether you have been able to put your values into action. Have you been able to live by your value system?

Select three values from the previous exercise that you rated as very important. Contemplate ways to put each value into practice. For example, if helping others is a value, how can you volunteer your time to help a cause, friend, or neighbor in need?

In the first column, list the three values you selected, and describe how you plan to put each into action. In the second column, list three obstacles that might get in the way of putting your values into action.

VALUES	OBSTACLES

In what ways do you want to grow or become stronger in these values?

Strength in My Scars

The scars of our childhood will remain with us, whether we like it or not. What happened to you in your childhood shaped who you are today, but you can work with what has happened, process your emotions, and learn how to deal with the scars. Finding strength in your scars will allow you to view your situation from a different perspective. In the space, write about what your experience as a child of a narcissistic mother has provided you with. How can you use what has happened to you to help others?

_____

_____

_____

_____

_____

_____

_____

_____

_____

_____

_____

_____

_____

_____

_____

Five-Senses Soothing

Self-soothing can help you manage your emotions and feel grounded. As you work through the exercises in this book, you may need to stop and gather yourself. This practice has many benefits and is usually practiced by stimulating one or all of your five senses when you're feeling distressed, overwhelmed, or anxious. Try experimenting with these techniques until you find some that you are comfortable with.

Practice at least one of these self-soothing exercises this week. When you practice, make sure you're doing it mindfully and breathing calmly. Afterward, consider how it felt.

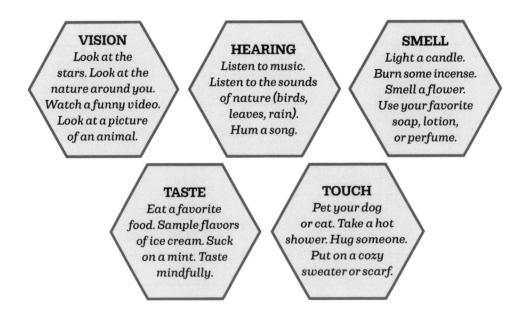

VISION
Look at the stars. Look at the nature around you. Watch a funny video. Look at a picture of an animal.

HEARING
Listen to music. Listen to the sounds of nature (birds, leaves, rain). Hum a song.

SMELL
Light a candle. Burn some incense. Smell a flower. Use your favorite soap, lotion, or perfume.

TASTE
Eat a favorite food. Sample flavors of ice cream. Suck on a mint. Taste mindfully.

TOUCH
Pet your dog or cat. Take a hot shower. Hug someone. Put on a cozy sweater or scarf.

Creating a Support Network

One of the questions I ask clients when I meet them is "Who is in your support network?" Humans are meant to support and assist each other. Narcissistic parents are well versed in isolation and division, so learning to ask for help and support may feel uncomfortable for you. You may feel as though you don't deserve the support, you don't want to burden anyone, or you can figure all of this out on your own. After all, haven't you always figured things out for yourself?

As you move through recovery and work on breaking the cycle of abuse, it's critical to create a support network of people you can depend on. This may include family, friends, therapists, mentors, fellow survivors, and your religious or spiritual community. Let's first review the types of support available.

TYPES OF SUPPORT	DEFINITION	EXAMPLE
Emotional	Nurturing support	A friend gives you a hug when you're having a bad day.
Functional	Support for practical problems	Your neighbor brings in your mail when you're out of town.
Advisory	Information or advice	Your therapist helps you resolve a dilemma you're having.
Companionship	Sense of belonging	Your neighborhood creates a meal train when you break your leg.

List three people you would include in your support system. Then describe how each person can support or help you with your emotional, functional, advisory, and companionship needs.

1. _____

2. _____

3. _____

Creating a Mantra

Look how far you've come! You have every reason to be proud of all you have accomplished in your recovery and healing. Now it's time to create your own mantra—a short saying or phrase you can use when you are meditating, relaxing, or enjoying quiet time alone.

Keep in mind that a good mantra is short, powerful, and motivational. Follow these steps to create your own mantra.

Reflect. Take fifteen to twenty minutes and reflect on what you want in your life moving forward. Consider your struggles, your desires, your achievements, and what defines you. Use the space to write down your thoughts and notes.

_____

_____

_____

_____

_____

_____

Examine. What have you discovered about yourself during your recovery that gives you confidence to overcome challenges? Write about this.

_____

_____

_____

_____

_____

_____

Create. Create a saying, quote, or message that makes you feel self-assured, confident, and strong. Keep it short so you can easily remember it.

For example:

Positive mind, positive life

Challenges create a better me

I am enough

_____

_____

_____

_____

_____

_____

Practice this daily.

Code of Well-Being

As you have learned during your work in recovery, children of narcissists rely on the rules, values, and beliefs of the narcissist rather than their own. This exercise will help you create a core set of rules for your well-being. To do this, review the example beliefs in the thought bubbles. Then, in the empty thought bubbles on the following page, write down beliefs you have learned during your journey. Use words that empower and guide you.

Copy your rules, print them out, and keep them in a place where you can see them every day. Then, as you think of new ones, draw new thought bubbles and write them in.

Why is each of these beliefs important to you?

_____

_____

_____

_____

_____

_____

_____

→

My Recovery Support

The journey of self-discovery, recovery, and healing should not be embarked on alone. In this chapter, we discussed the importance of a support network. Reflect on some of the people you listed as your supporters in "Creating a Support Network" (page 119). Think about the relationship you have with each person, and describe why each relationship is meaningful to you. Write about how they have impacted you through your journey of recovery and how you may have affected them, too.

_____

_____

_____

_____

_____

_____

_____

_____

_____

_____

_____

_____

_____

_____

_____

_____

Body Scan

Body scanning can help you calm down when you are experiencing any type of stress. This technique will help you check in with yourself during times of stress and throughout the process of healing.

1. Start by getting comfortable, in a seated position, if possible. Close your eyes.

2. Notice how your feet feel on the floor. Slowly, focus on your ankles and then your knees, thighs, and stomach. Identify weight, pressure, tension, heat, and any other sensations as you move up your body.

3. When you feel any tension, take a deep breath and exhale as you release it. When you feel each body part relax, move to the next one.

4. When you finish with your lower body, do the same with your upper body: chest, shoulders, arms, and hands. During your body scan, think about including internal organs like your stomach, heart, and lungs.

5. Notice your neck and throat. Soften them. Relax.

6. Release any tension in your jaw. Relax your face and facial muscles.

7. Be aware of your whole body as best you can. Take one more deep breath. When you're ready, open your eyes.

> **I am a valuable and important person, worthy of the respect of others and, more important, myself.**

Key Takeaways

As you have come to realize in this chapter, breaking the cycle is more than just a choice. It requires taking action, changing your thinking, and understanding your personal story. It requires a great deal of reflection on both yourself and your family. You may have made some big discoveries while working in this chapter—some may have been difficult and even painful, but these discoveries empower you to understand yourself better. Life changes are never easy, but developing healthy skills and abilities will allow you to create a new cycle of respect for yourself and others around you. Once you expand your self-esteem, put your values into action, and become secure in your beliefs about yourself, the cycle of abuse will be destroyed.

Keep the following in mind:

→ Understanding your family's trauma and how it affected you can help you break the cycle of abuse.

→ Knowledge of what a healthy relationship is and means to you is a critical part of building your identity.

→ Identifying your values and beliefs allows you to put them into action and live life on your terms.

→ You can use your personal mantra to help you stay on track and reduce negative thoughts.

CHAPTER SIX

Taking Care of You

Yes, mental health is key, but did you know that working on your physical health, social health, and spiritual health is equally important to your recovery? Overall well-being is tied to all areas and dimensions of our lives, and so is good self-care.

In this chapter, you'll explore how well you take care of yourself. It is unlikely that the skills of self-care were discussed with you while you were a child, so it's okay if you are not doing as much in this arena as you should. You'll learn valuable skills as you work through this chapter. Discovering your purpose and exploring your spirituality are important parts of recovery; in fact, they are keys to unlocking the mystery that is you. Now that you understand how to manage your emotions and work on your identity, let's take it a step further and explore your purpose, goals, and accomplishments. Finally, you'll sum it all up by looking at your healing from A to Z.

Bridgit's Boundary Work

Bridgit is a thirty-eight-year-old married woman who was recently released from inpatient psychiatric care. No stranger to counseling or psychiatric care, Bridgit had been fighting mental health issues for decades. Her first marriage ended in divorce after several years of abusive behavior from her husband. Bridgit had recently remarried. She was excited but somewhat cautious about her new marriage, since she and her new husband had only known each other for three months before they married.

Bridgit's childhood was wrought with dysfunction. Her mother and father divorced when Bridgit was a teenager, and she rarely saw her father after the divorce. Bitter about the divorce, Bridgit's mother continually disparaged Bridgit's father in front of her and her brother. Bridgit was also blamed for most of the problems in the house. She believes it was because she looks like her father—her mother would take her anger toward her father out on her.

Bridgit knew she needed to make some changes and break away from her mother or at least establish some boundaries with her. Recently, Bridgit's mother invited her and her new husband over for dinner. Bridgit was apprehensive but decided to go and practice some of the boundaries she had been learning in therapy. She phoned her mother the day before and communicated that if her mother was rude and disrespectful to her, she and her husband would leave.

Bridgit was proud of herself for setting the boundaries. They went for dinner, and surprisingly, her mother was reasonably nice. This motivated Bridgit to work on some other issues, including taking better care of herself physically, decluttering her home, and focusing on herself.

Brief Relaxation

You can't have too many different relaxation techniques in your toolkit. Benefits of relaxation include decreases in blood pressure, heart rate, and respiration rate, making it an ideal tool to use to manage distressing emotions. Over time, a regular practice of relaxation can produce an overall feeling of relaxation in your life. As you assess your self-care skills, practice this brief relaxation method whenever you get the chance.

1. Get comfortable.

2. Count backward from ten to zero, silently saying each number as you exhale.

3. Relax more deeply, and go deeper and deeper into a state of relaxation as you count. Feel a physical and emotional calm take over as you let go.

4. As you continue counting down with each breath, feel the tension leave your body as you become limp.

5. When you reach zero, feel yourself being completely relaxed, tranquil and serene, safe and secure, and peacefully calm.

> **I love myself just the way I am.**

My Self-Care Assessment

Self-care is the practice of actively taking care of your physical self in combination with your mental health. This wellness assessment works well for survivors of abuse who have not learned to take care of themselves because it shines a light on areas to work on. Review and rate yourself from 0 to 5 in each area.

0 = almost never   **1** = rarely   **2** = sometimes
3 = frequently   **4** = most often   **5** = always

Physical Self-Care

I eat healthy foods.

0   1   2   3   4   5

I move my body through exercise.

0   1   2   3   4   5

I get enough sleep.

0   1   2   3   4   5

I participate in activities I enjoy.

0   1   2   3   4   5

I eat regularly.

0   1   2   3   4   5

Emotional Self-Care

I recognize my strengths and accomplishments.

0   1   2   3   4   5

I laugh regularly.

0   1   2   3   4   5

I talk about my problems.

0   1   2   3   4   5

I take time off from work, school, or other obligations when needed.

0   1   2   3   4   5

I relax and/or journal when needed.

0   1   2   3   4   5

Spiritual Self-Care

I make time for reflection.

0   1   2   3   4   5

I spend time in nature.

0   1   2   3   4   5

I have a spiritual connection or community.

0   1   2   3   4   5

I identify what is meaningful to me and notice its place in my life.

0   1   2   3   4   5

I meditate.

0   1   2   3   4   5

→

Social Self-Care

I ask others for help when I need it.

    0   1   2   3   4   5

I spend time with people I enjoy.

    0   1   2   3   4   5

I meet new people.

    0   1   2   3   4   5

I keep in touch with family and friends.

    0   1   2   3   4   5

I spend quality time with my loved ones.

    0   1   2   3   4   5

Plan Your Self-Care Practices

In the last exercise, you assessed how well you are doing in different areas of your self-care. In this exercise, use the self-care wheel to plan your self-care practices. This wheel identifies the physical, emotional, social, and spiritual aspects of self-care. Use the following blank self-care wheel to fill in each aspect of your self-care that needs attention. You can refer to "My Self-Care Assessment" (page 130) for ideas if needed.

Keep this wheel in mind as you plan your daily self-care activities.

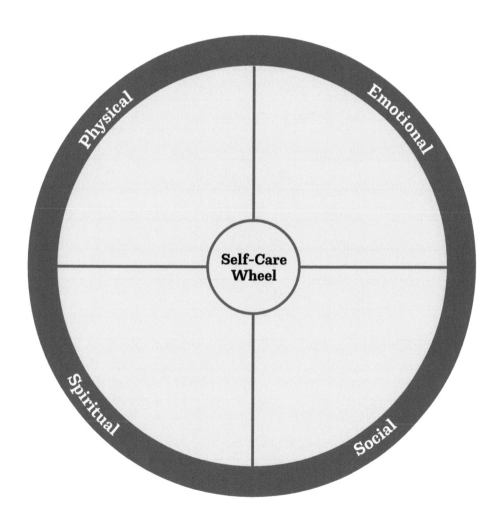

My New Understanding

Has this chapter challenged you to look at self-care from a new perspective? Perhaps you didn't realize that self-care had so many dimensions. Consider what you have learned so far about your self-care behaviors. What are three behaviors that no longer serve you and do not support your self-care? How can you stop doing these things?

_____

_____

_____

_____

_____

_____

_____

_____

_____

_____

_____

_____

_____

_____

_____

_____

Contemplative Reading

Contemplative reading is a practice of scriptural reading, meditation, and prayer. Acts of contemplation calm the mind and spirit and allow you to focus your thoughts and let your mind wander. Contemplative reading involves reading a short passage and then quietly reflecting on it. Follow along with these guidelines to practice this technique.

1. Select a short piece of inspirational writing or an object that has meaning to you.

2. Slowly read the passage or look at the object and ask yourself, *Which word or phrase do I connect with right now?* or *Why does this passage/object have meaning to me?*

3. Pick a word or phrase or part of the passage/object that you feel drawn to rather than something you feel like you should choose.

4. Slowly read the piece or look at the object again.

5. Ask yourself, *How does this word, phrase, or object relate to my life right now?*

6. Think about the thoughts that you have.

7. Notice what you are paying attention to. It's okay if nothing comes to mind.

8. Slowly read the piece or look at the object again one more time.

9. Ask yourself, *What am I being asked? Am I being asked to trust? Accept? Or do something?*

10. Reflect on this practice. Ask yourself, *What are my thoughts, feelings, and emotions about this practice?*

My Spirituality

Spirituality is an important part of well-being. Narcissistic abuse can have a significant impact on a person's spirituality. Injuries to your spirituality as a result of abuse may have led to feelings of guilt and anger, fear of death, and a belief that life is unfair. Conversely, healthy spirituality can lead to resiliency and can help survivors of abuse cope, both emotionally and physically.

For many people, spirituality can be a confusing concept. You may ask yourself, "What does it mean to be spiritual? How can this concept help me in my recovery?" Spiritual well-being is about finding a sense of purpose and meaning in your life. There are countless aspects of spiritual health, including self-reflection, connecting with nature, meditation, and so much more. Being spiritually healthy means you understand your values and you have inner peace and a greater purpose for your life than just "being." In the spaces that follow, answer questions about where you are with your spirituality and how you got here.

What do I currently believe about spirituality?

_____

_____

_____

_____

_____

How have my life experiences influenced my spiritual beliefs?

_____

_____

_____

_____

_____

What might be preventing me from developing a more meaningful spiritual life?

_____

_____

_____

_____

_____

What three things could I do to make my spiritual life more meaningful?

1. _____

2. _____

3. _____

Self-Care Obstacles

You have now assessed and created a plan to improve or add to your self-care. With any new endeavor, it pays to think about possible resistance or obstacles that could get in the way of your self-care. Even the most devoted person might encounter obstacles or resistance to change. Reflect on the coping strategies and self-care tools you have discovered in the previous activities. What's working? What isn't working?

What messages do you tell yourself about self-care?

_____

_____

_____

_____

_____

_____

_____

How could you improve these messages?

_____

_____

_____

_____

_____

_____

_____

Are there obstacles to carrying out your self-care plan? If yes, what are they?

☐ Time   ☐ Fear

☐ Money   ☐ Other: _____

☐ Lack of motivation

In what ways can you overcome any obstacles to your self-care? Can any of your supporters help you overcome the obstacles? (Refer to your supporters from the "Creating a Support Network" exercise on page 119.) If yes, which ones, and how?

_____

_____

_____

_____

_____

_____

_____

_____

_____

_____

_____

_____

_____

_____

My Self-Care Goals

Goal-setting is the practice of identifying things you want to achieve and making a plan to get there. Setting self-care goals allows you to focus on choosing things that will benefit your mind, body, and soul. Some benefits of setting self-care goals include personal accountability, increased productivity, improved self-esteem, and a better understanding of yourself.

The first column in the table lists areas of your life that involve self-care. In the second column, write down what you do well in each of these areas. In the third column, write down how you can improve in each area. In the fourth column, set a goal for improvement in each area. Write down what comes to mind.

	WHAT I DO WELL	WHERE I NEED TO IMPROVE	MY GOAL
FAMILY			
FRIENDS			
WORK/SCHOOL			
PHYSICAL HEALTH			
MENTAL HEALTH			
SPIRITUAL HEALTH			

Self-Care and Trauma

Trauma can warp your ability to protect your sense of wellness. Adults who experienced trauma in childhood may find it difficult to practice self-care regularly or even recognize what self-care is. You may have thought you were practicing self-care when you were really just coping. How has your experience with your mother affected your self-care practice? Reflect and write about how your trauma has affected your ability to practice self-care.

_____

_____

_____

_____

_____

_____

_____

_____

_____

_____

_____

_____

_____

_____

_____

_____

Greet the Day

This practice will allow you to align your breathing rhythm with the rhythms of a new day.

Try to practice this outside if you can, but you can also practice inside. You will be sending seven breaths of greeting to seven directions: east, west, south, north, above, below, and within.

1. Standing or sitting, face the direction of the dawn (east). Take deep breaths to relax your body. Notice your feet and their contact with the ground. Feel your connection to the earth.

2. Give thanks for the previous day.

3. Feel the air around you. Notice the breath and air entering your nose and lungs. Observe your body as it takes in the air of the new day.

4. Breathing slowly, raise your arms above your head toward the sun. Inhale and give thanks. Notice the air moving through your body.

5. Continue to breathe in and exhale.

6. Now, turn clockwise to face the south. Breathe in and exhale.

7. Turn to face west. Breathe in and exhale.

8. Turn to face north. Breathe in and exhale.

9. Turn once more to face the east. Raise your head toward the sky (above), breathe in, and then exhale.

10. Bow your head to acknowledge the earth (below). Breathe in and exhale.

11. Lower your arms and cross them over your heart. Breathe in (within) and exhale.

12. Enjoy this state of peace and calm for a few moments. Resume your day.

My Resiliency Plan

We've explored how resiliency is the ability to recover from difficulties in life. Resilient people rely on social support, coping skills, wisdom, and problem-solving. This exercise will help you build a personal resiliency plan, which you can use to help you combat any future challenges.

Think about a problem or challenge you are currently having in your life. Follow the prompts to fill in the boxes.

In the first box, list people in your life who have supported you—for example, an old friend, a teacher, or another family member. Write down whom you called on for support.

```
Support
```

Think of the ways that you helped yourself cope with negative thoughts and feelings during the difficult time. In the following box, write down the strategies you used.

```
Coping Skills
```

What thoughts and beliefs helped you "bounce back" from this problem? Think about any wisdom or insight that helped you. Was it a song, a quote, or insight from a respected person you know? Write down your wisdom in the box.

```
Wisdom
```

What problem-solving skills did you use? Did you seek out new information, plan ahead, compromise, or ask others for help? Write down the problem-solving skills you used in the box.

```
Problem-Solving
```

Congratulations! You have created a resiliency plan. The next time you find yourself in a difficult or challenging situation, remember the steps you took to get through it. Then give yourself a hand!

Discovering My Purpose

This long journey to healing and recovery presents the perfect opportunity to think about your purpose in life. Finding and knowing your purpose creates meaning in your life. It gives you a better idea of who you are, where you fit in, and what you want to accomplish in life. Knowing your purpose will give you a guiding light to follow and ensure that you have a good reason for being here and a better reason to recover and heal. Complete the following questions to discover your purpose.

If you know your life purpose, write it here:

_____

_____

_____

_____

If you are unsure, answer the following questions and see where they lead you. What are your thoughts about the work you are doing now? Are you fulfilled?

_____

_____

_____

_____

Do you have any interest in continuing your education? If so, in what area?

_____

_____

_____

_____

Are there any hobbies or interests you want to pursue? If so, describe them.

_____

_____

_____

_____

If you could accomplish anything in the next year, what would it be?

_____

_____

_____

_____

If you could change one thing in your life that would allow you to achieve your purpose, what would it be?

_____

_____

_____

_____

Hopefully, after completing this exercise, you have had the chance to think more about your purpose in life. If you are still contemplating it, don't give up. Finding your purpose can be a rewarding journey all its own.

My Personal Accomplishments

Tracking your accomplishments is a form of self-care. People who can recognize their strengths tend to be happier and have greater self-esteem. From the time you were born, you were accomplishing things. For this exercise, consider some things you have accomplished in your journey just this past week. Consider how you think, how you manage feelings, the difficulties in your life, and the changes you have made. You may choose to use a notebook or journal to keep track of the accomplishments you will continue to make in the months and years to come.

Things I accomplished this week:

_____

_____

_____

How long I have been working on them:

_____

_____

_____

These accomplishments were important because:

_____

_____

_____

Skills I learned, challenges I overcame, or problems I solved this week:

_____

_____

_____

Good feedback I got this week:

_____

_____

_____

One thing I'm proud that I did this week:

_____

_____

_____

One thing I'd like to accomplish next week:

_____

_____

_____

My Gifts

We have spent a great deal of time addressing the things that your mother did wrong. It's important to remember that no one is all good or all bad, including your mother. You now have a better sense of yourself and what self-love really is, and the future is yours to determine. Consider the idea that your mother likely passed along interests, abilities, and knowledge to you. Write about the talents that your mother gave you.

_____

_____

_____

_____

_____

_____

_____

_____

_____

_____

_____

_____

_____

_____

_____

_____

Awaken Compassion

An ancient Buddhist practice known as *tonglen* teaches us "sending and taking." As we breathe in, we take in others' pain, and as we breathe out, we send them relief. This practice will awaken your compassion and help you learn to feel love both for yourself and for others. There are four stages to *tonglen*.

1. Rest your mind for a second or two. Try to connect with your heart and mind. Breathe.

2. Begin visualizing.

    a. Breathe in feelings of heat, darkness, and heaviness. Breathe out feelings of coolness, brightness, and light.

    b. Breathe in completely. Take in the pain of others.

    c. Exhale. Send out positive energy and thoughts.

    d. Continue until your visualization is synchronized with your breaths.

3. Focus on a real, painful situation. It can be for someone you care about and want to help or pain you are experiencing yourself.

    a. Breathe in the pain and discomfort.

    b. Exhale with positive energy.

4. Awaken your compassion.

    a. Make the taking in and sending out bigger.

    b. Extend it to all people, not just one person.

    c. Breathe in the pain of someone who hurt you, and send them relief.

Reflect on the practice. How was it for you?

_____

_____

My Recovery Alphabet

What if you could describe your journey of recovery using every letter of the alphabet? What words would you use? Use each letter of the alphabet as inspiration to come up with one to three words that describe you and your healing journey. For example:

A. accomplishment, assertive, able

B. brave, bold, beautiful

C. caring, committed

D. daring, dedicated, determined

Now, develop your own alphabet.

A. _____

B. _____

C. _____

D. _____

E. _____

F. _____

G. _____

H. _____

I. _____

J. _____

K. _____

L. _____

M. _____

N. _____

O. _____

P. _____

Q. _____

R. _____

S. _____

T. _____

U. _____

V. _____

W. _____

X. _____

Y. _____

Z. _____

S Is for Survivor

At the beginning of your journey of recovery, it may have been difficult to view yourself as a survivor. Now, you know that overcoming the effects of abuse requires determination, strength, and courage. Moving from being a victim to being a survivor will be one of the biggest accomplishments you will achieve. You may still be contemplating where you stand with feeling like a survivor. That is certainly understandable. There may be days, weeks, or even months when you are unsure of how you feel about your recovery. Just remember: The fact that you decided to work through this book makes you a survivor. The feelings and thoughts connected to being a victim are negative and self-defeating. The feelings and thoughts connected to being a survivor are positive and uplifting—embrace them.

In this exercise, review the following list of words and phrases that describe either a victim or a survivor. Label each phrase with "V" for victim or "S" for survivor.

Focused on pain	_____	Depressed	_____
Enjoys living	_____	Isolated	_____
Wants understanding	_____	Confident	_____
No energy	_____	Enjoys living	_____
Helpless	_____	Overcomes pain	_____
Optimistic	_____	Hopeless	_____
Lives in the past	_____	Lets go of anger	_____
Empowered	_____	Trusting	_____
Defeated	_____	Fearful	_____
Bitter	_____	Lives in the present	_____

After reviewing the previous list, do you see yourself more as a victim or as a survivor? Why?

_____

_____

_____

Which three words most accurately described you *before* working on your recovery from abuse?

_____

_____

_____

Which three words most accurately describe you *now*?

_____

_____

_____

What has helped you the most in moving toward becoming a survivor?

_____

_____

_____

Keep Calm and Cope Along Cards

You have worked on and learned a great deal during your journey of healing. This exercise is intended to remind you of the knowledge you've acquired as you move through the different circumstances that will come your way. This tool is helpful to remind you that you now have the coping skills to deal with your emotions, anxious thoughts, and stressful situations as they occur in your life.

Complete each card with a coping skill that you can use, detailing how to use it and how it will help. Add a member of your support network to remind you that you can call on this person if you need support. Take a picture of each card with your phone, and save them as handy reminders. You can also copy these templates onto a separate sheet of paper and carry them with you.

Coping skill: _____

_____

How to use: _____

_____

How it will help: _____

_____

Support contact: _____

Coping skill: _____

_____

How to use: _____

_____

How it will help: _____

_____

Support contact: _____

Coping skill: _____

_____

How to use: _____

_____

How it will help: _____

_____

Support contact: _____

Coping skill: _____

_____

How to use: _____

_____

How it will help: _____

_____

Support contact: _____

Thank You

All the work you've completed is a profound achievement. It takes a great deal of courage to face and process the experiences you have worked through during this journey. Congratulations! Write a thank-you note to yourself for everything you're doing for your well-being. Include all the things you would say to your best friend if they had completed the same journey.

_____

_____

_____

_____

_____

_____

_____

_____

_____

_____

_____

_____

_____

_____

_____

_____

_____

_____

Counting Breaths

Concentration is a key to meditation, since it will help you reduce distractions. This structured meditation helps you continuously focus on your breathing by counting breaths.

1. Find a comfortable place to sit.

2. Focus on breathing in and out, slowly and smoothly. Each time you breathe out, silently count the breath. Count to ten or higher.

3. Each time your thoughts and focus drift, bring them back to your breathing and counting. If you get caught up in the distraction, don't judge yourself. Simply return to counting and relax.

4. If you lose track of counting, start over at one or a round number like ten or twenty.

5. After practicing counting breaths for a while, let go of counting and concentrate on breathing in and out.

6. Continue this for ten minutes or up to thirty minutes.

> **I am optimistic about life because I'm in charge of how I feel, and I choose serenity.**

Key Takeaways

Self-care is about taking care of all parts of you. Hopefully, after working through the exercises in this chapter, you can see what holistic self-care can and should look like. I frequently encourage my clients to "be their own cheerleader." No one else is going to support you more than you will. This means not only taking care of daily tasks, like brushing your teeth or taking a shower, but also taking care of your physical health, emotional health, social health, and spiritual health. Only you can do these things, and in this chapter, you obtained the skills to do just that. Self-care is not the equivalent of being selfish. It's about providing yourself with the necessary attention to continue being the compassionate, empathetic person you are.

Keep the following in mind:

→ Self-care involves all dimensions of health for a balanced life.

→ Setting and keeping goals is an ongoing process for a healthy, balanced, growth-filled life.

→ Discovering your purpose can provide a guiding light for how to live your life.

→ By regularly identifying your accomplishments, you offer yourself recognition of your worth and growth.

→ A focus on spirituality in any way can spark growth, satisfaction, and meaning in your life.

A Final Note

You did it! Seeking help, working on your mental health and well-being, and allowing yourself to journey through the difficult emotions that come with abuse are accomplishments well worth celebrating. My hope for you and all of my clients is to find a life that includes peace, joy, and contentment. At times, these may seem elusive, particularly as the daughter of a narcissistic mother. My wish is that you have come to see yourself from a new perspective with the help of this workbook.

Your journey may be just beginning, but this workbook is one tool you have in a toolbox that will help you continue to grow and discover and accept yourself for all the wonderful things you are. Please use this book as a reference whenever you find yourself needing reassurance or reinforcement. Remember, if you have worked with this book, there are many others out there who have as well. Finding support from others who have gone through similar circumstances will be an important part of your recovery.

Remind yourself how learning to identify and process your emotions has helped you discover what is important to you. This is a skill that nobody can take away from you. You've become more aware of how your experience changed the way you think, but your new skills to help replace negative thoughts have allowed you to correct those unhelpful thinking patterns. You now have the knowledge and understanding to protect yourself and even choose yourself first. This is good! Healthy boundaries will allow you to develop healthy relationships. With these boundaries, you can communicate effectively to establish and keep meaningful, rewarding relationships.

Knowledge is power in your recovery. Knowing your story helps you understand how the things in your life have affected you, both negatively and positively. Remember to always be your own cheerleader. You're responsible for your own happiness, and nourishing this concept will benefit you. You are a very special person just as you are.

You have taken on this challenge, and for that I commend you. It's not easy to face a history of abuse and neglect at the hands of a parent, but you did, and you survived. As you continue to move through your journey, if you find yourself stuck or if you need additional support, please consider seeking the help of a licensed therapist. A therapist can help you sort through issues and difficulties that you may encounter along the way. Please remember one last thing: I am proud of you!

Resources

Books

Becoming the Narcissist's Nightmare: How to Devalue and Discard the Narcissist while Supplying Yourself by Shahida Arabi

Children of the Self-Absorbed: A Grown-Up's Guide to Getting Over Narcissistic Parents by Nina W. Brown, EdD, LPC

Facing Codependence by Pia Mellody, Andrea Wells Miller, and J. Keith Miller

Motherless Daughters by Hope Edelman

Mothers Who Can't Love: A Healing Guide for Daughters by Susan Forward and Donna Frazier Glynn

Toxic Parents: Overcoming Their Hurtful Legacy and Reclaiming Your Life by Susan Forward and Craig Buck

An Unsuspecting Child by Marylee Martin

Will I Ever Be Good Enough? by Karyl McBride

Websites

Narcissistic Abuse Recovery
queenbeeing.com
A website created by an abuse survivor who is now a certified trauma counselor offering videos, articles, and podcasts to assist with recovery

Narcissistic Abuse Support
narcissistabusesupport.com
A helpful website full of resources, online groups, and workshops on narcissistic abuse

YouTube Channels

Dr. Ramani Durvasula
youtube.com/channel/UC9Qixc77KhCo88E5muxUjmA
Videos by a clinical psychologist and author whose mission is to help people understand narcissism

Lisa A. Romano Breakthrough Life Coach Inc.
youtube.com/c/lisaaromano1
Videos full of helpful information addressing narcissistic abuse and codependency

Melanie Tonia Evans
youtube.com/user/MelanieToniaEvans/videos
Videos based on personal experience and spiritual understanding to help people recover from narcissistic abuse

Facebook Forums

Narcissist Abuse and Recovery Support
facebook.com/groups/189213149802053
A private forum for people who have been in relationships with narcissists and want to share their stories

Narcissistic Abuse and Toxic Relationship Forum
facebook.com/freefromtoxic
A forum moderated by a licensed psychotherapist, which provides support and education to people who are recovering from narcissistic abuse

References

American Psychiatric Association. 2022. *Diagnostic and Statistical Manual of Mental Disorders, Fifth Edition, Text Revision (DSM-5-TR™)*. Arlington, TX: American Psychiatric Association Publishing.

Arabi, Shahida. 2016. *Becoming the Narcissist's Nightmare: How to Devalue and Discard the Narcissist While Supplying Yourself*. SCW Archer Publishing.

Arabi, Shahida. 2019. *Healing the Adult Children of Narcissists: Essays on the Invisible War Zone*. SCW Archer Publishing.

Bourne, Edmund J. 2011. *The Anxiety & Phobia Workbook*. 5th ed. Oakland, CA: New Harbinger Publications.

Bowlby, John. 1979. "The Bowlby-Ainsworth Attachment Theory." *The Behavioral and Brain Sciences* 2 (4): 637–38. doi.org/10.1017/s0140525x00064955.

Brown, Brené. *Atlas of the Heart: Mapping Meaningful Connection and the Language of Human Experience*. Random House Publishing Group, 2021.

Brown, Nina W. *Children of the Self-Absorbed: A Grown-Up's Guide to Getting over Narcissistic Parents*. United Kingdom: New Harbinger Publications, 2008.

Brummelman, Eddie, Sander Thomaes, Stefanie A. Nelemans, Bram Orobio de Castro, Geertjan Overbeek, and Brad J. Bushman. 2015. "Origins of Narcissism in Children." *Proceedings of the National Academy of Sciences of the United States of America* 112 (12): 3659–62. doi.org/10.1073/pnas.1420870112.

Caligor, Eve, Kenneth N. Levy, and Frank E. Yeomans. 2015. "Narcissistic Personality Disorder: Diagnostic and Clinical Challenges." *The American Journal of Psychiatry* 172 (5): 415–22. doi.org/10.1176/appi.ajp.2014.14060723.

Carlson, Eve B., Lita Furby, Judith Armstrong, and Jennifer Shlaes. 1997. "A Conceptual Framework for the Long-Term Psychological Effects of Traumatic Childhood Abuse." *Child Maltreatment* 2 (3): 272–95. doi.org/10.1177/1077559597002003009.

Cartwright, Mark. 2017. "Narcissus." *World History Encyclopedia*. worldhistory.org /Narcissus.

Chapman, Alexander L., Matthew T. Tull, and Kim L. Gratz. 2017. *The Cognitive Behavioral Coping Skills Workbook for PTSD: Overcome Fear and Anxiety and Reclaim Your Life*. Oakland, CA: New Harbinger Publications.

Cherry, Kendra. n.d. "Uninvolved Parenting and Its Effects on Children." Verywell Mind. Accessed March 19, 2022. verywellmind.com/what-is-uninvolved-parenting -2794958.

Chödrön, Pema. 2022. "How to Practice Tonglen." Lion's Roar. January 14, 2022. lionsroar.com/how-to-practice-tonglen.

Comito, Theresa. 2020. *The Emotional Abuse Recovery Workbook: Breaking the Cycle of Psychological Violence*. Rockridge Press.

Fisher, Janina. 2021. *Transforming the Living Legacy of Trauma: A Workbook for Survivors and Therapists*. Pesi Publishing & Media.

Fjelstad, Margalis. 2019. *Healing from a Narcissistic Relationship: A Caretaker's Guide to Recovery, Empowerment, and Transformation*. Lanham, MD: Rowman & Littlefield.

Fox, Daniel J. 2020. *Antisocial, Narcissistic, and Borderline Personality Disorders: A New Conceptualization of Development, Reinforcement, Expression, and Treatment*. London, England: Routledge.

Fronsdal, Gil. 2008. *The Issue at Hand: Essays on Buddhist Mindfulness Practice*. Insight Meditation Center.

"Greeting the Day by Jack Angelo." n.d. Spiritualityandpractice.com. Accessed March 20, 2022. spiritualityandpractice.com/practices/practices/view/28869/greeting -the-day.

Hayes, S. C., K. D. Strosahl, and K. G. Wilson. 1999. *Acceptance and Commitment Therapy; An Experiential Approach to Behavior Change*. New York: Guildford Press.

Johnson, Sharon L. 2017. *Therapist's Guide to Clinical Intervention: The 1-2-3's of Treatment Planning*. 3rd ed. San Diego, CA: Academic Press.

Jongsma, Arthur E. 2006. *The Complete Adult Psychotherapy Treatment Planner: WITH Adult Psychotherapy Homework Planner, 2r.E.* 4th ed. Chichester, England: John Wiley & Sons.

Lee, Tae-Ho, Yang Qu, and Eva H. Telzer. 2017. "Love Flows Downstream: Mothers' and Children's Neural Representation Similarity in Perceiving Distress of Self and Family." *Social Cognitive and Affective Neuroscience* 12 (12): 1916–27. doi.org/10.1093/scan/nsx125.

Levy, Kenneth N., Preeti Chauhan, John F. Clarkin, Rachel H. Wasserman, and Joseph S. Reynoso. 2009. "Narcissistic Pathology: Empirical Approaches." *Psychiatric Annals* 39 (4): 203–13. doi.org/10.3928/00485713-20090401-03.

Linehan, Marsha M. 2014. *DBT® Skills Training Handouts and Worksheets.* 2nd ed. New York, NY: Guilford Publications.

Luo, Yu L. L., Huajian Cai, and Hairong Song. 2014. "A Behavioral Genetic Study of Intrapersonal and Interpersonal Dimensions of Narcissism." *PloS One* 9 (4): e93403. doi.org/10.1371/journal.pone.0093403.

McBride, Karyl. 2009. *Will I Ever Be Good Enough?: Healing the Daughters of Narcissistic Mothers.* New York, NY: Simon & Schuster.

McElvaney, Jeanne. *Healing Insights: Effects of Abuse for Adults Abused as Children.* Createspace Independent Publishing Platform, 2013.

McKay, Matthew, and Jeffrey C. Wood. 2019. *The Dialectical Behavior Therapy Skills Workbook the Dialectical Behavior Therapy Skills Workbook: Practical DBT Exercises for Learning Mindfulness, Interpersonal Effectiveness, Emotion Regulation, and Distress Tolerance.* Oakland, CA: New Harbinger Publications.

Miles, Gabrielle J., and Andrew J. P. Francis. 2014. "Narcissism: Is Parenting Style to Blame, or Is There X-Chromosome Involvement?" *Psychiatry Research* 219 (3): 712–13. doi.org/10.1016/j.psychres.2014.07.003.

Miller, Joshua D., Donald R. Lynam, Courtland S. Hyatt, and W. Keith Campbell. 2017. "Controversies in Narcissism." *Annual Review of Clinical Psychology* 13 (1): 291–315. doi.org/10.1146/annurev-clinpsy-032816-045244.

Nenadić, Igor, Carsten Lorenz, and Christian Gaser. 2021. "Narcissistic Personality Traits and Prefrontal Brain Structure." *Scientific Reports* 11 (1): 15707. doi.org/10.1038/s41598-021-94920-z.

Nilon, Lorraine. *Breaking Free from the Chains of Silence: A Respectful Exploration into the Ramifications of Paedophilic Abuse.* Insight and Awareness Pty, Ltd., 2017.

Pearlman, Laurie Anne, and Karen W. Saakvitne. 1996. *Transforming the Pain: A Workbook on Vicarious Traumatization.* New York, NY: W. W. Norton.

Pedrick, Cherry, and Bruce M. Hyman. 2005. *The OCD Workbook: Your Guide to Breaking Free from Obsessive-Compulsive Disorder.* 2nd ed. Oakland, CA: New Harbinger Publications.

Ronningstam, Elsa. 2016. "New Insights into Narcissistic Personality Disorder." *Psychiatric Times* 33.

Schnall, Marianne. 2009. "An Interview with Maya Angelou: Maya Angelou Talks about Her New Book." *Psychology Today.* February 17, 2009. psychologytoday.com/us /blog/the-guest-room/200902/interview-maya-angelou.

Sperry, Len. 2016. *Handbook of Diagnosis and Treatment of DSM-5-TR Personality Disorders: Assessment, Case Conceptualization, and Treatment.* 3rd ed. London, England: Routledge.

"Spiritual Practice Worksheets to Support Your Well-Being in a Disaster or Emergency." n.d. Albertahealthservices.Ca. Accessed March 20, 2022. albertahealthservices .ca/assets/info/amh/if-amh-mhpip-spiritual-practices-workbook.pdf.

Stephens, Brenda. 2021. *Recovering from Narcissistic Mothers: A Daughter's Guide.* Rockridge Press.

Stinson, Frederick S., Deborah A. Dawson, Risë B. Goldstein, S. Patricia Chou, Boji Huang, Sharon M. Smith, W. June Ruan, et al. 2008. "Prevalence, Correlates, Disability, and Comorbidity of DSM-IV Narcissistic Personality Disorder: Results from the Wave 2 National Epidemiologic Survey on Alcohol and Related Conditions." *The Journal of Clinical Psychiatry* 69 (7): 1033–45. doi.org/10.4088/jcp.v69n0701.

Tawwab, Nedra Glover. 2021. *The Set Boundaries Workbook: Practical Exercises for Understanding Your Needs and Setting Healthy Limits.* London, England: Piatkus Books.

Van Dijk, Sheri. 2013. *DBT Made Simple: A Step-by-Step Guide to Dialectical Behavior Therapy*. Oakland, CA: New Harbinger Publications.

van Schie, Charlotte C., Heidi L. Jarman, Elizabeth Huxley, and Brin F. S. Grenyer. 2020. "Narcissistic Traits in Young People: Understanding the Role of Parenting and Maltreatment." *Borderline Personality Disorder and Emotion Dysregulation* 7 (1): 10. doi.org/10.1186/s40479-020-00125-7.

Wakefield, M. *Narcissistic Family Dynamics: Collected Essays: A Curated Selection of Essays on Narcissism in the Family*. Narcissistic Abuse Rehab, 2020.

Williams, Mary-Beth, and Soili Poijula. 2002. *The PTSD Workbook*. Oakland, CA: New Harbinger Publications.

Index

Acknowledgments

I would not be able to do the work that I do with survivors of narcissistic abuse without the courage of my clients. They are the true champions in their stories. I am beyond grateful for their bravery in sharing their experiences with me. I learn something new every time I meet with them, and I hope this book reflects all of the knowledge they have taught me.

About the Author

 **Ellen Biros, MS, LCSW, C-PD,** is a licensed clinical social worker and certified personality disorder treatment provider and has been practicing social work for over twenty years. She earned a master's in justice from American University in Washington, DC, and a master's in social work from the University of Georgia. In her private practice, she specializes in the assessment and treatment of individuals with personality disorders, substance abuse issues, and emotional regulation problems. She also provides clinical supervision for social workers seeking their clinical licensure.

Ellen is an adjunct faculty member and faculty liaison at Tulane University School of Social Work. She is a national continuing education speaker and has authored continuing education seminars including "Emotional Manipulators and Codependents: A Recipe for Disaster," "Unmasking Manipulative Relationships: Effective Strategies for Countering Covert Abuse," "Personality Disorders: The Challenges of the Hidden Agenda," and "Antisocial, Borderline, Narcissistic, and Histrionic: Effective Treatment for Cluster B Personality Disorders."